Sabina

Sabina

IN THE EYE OF THE STORM

Bella Kuligowska Zucker

Photos and images of documents contained in this book come originally from the family collection of Bella Kuligowska and Herman Zucker. Donated to the US Holocaust Memorial Museum and the Illinois Holocaust Museum and Education Center and used here with their courtesy. Images from the US Holocaust Memorial Museum appear on pages 118, 120, and 230–233. Images from the Illinois Holocaust Museum and Education Center appear on pages 18 and 155.
Map of Interwar Poland courtesy Gesher Galicia and Polona Digital Library.

First edition January 2018.
Paperback ISBN: 9781981953295

In memory of my beloved father, Bezalel Kuligowski,
my cherished mother, Chaya Kohn Kuligowska, and my
five precious brothers, Abraham, Israel, Benjamin, Joseph,
and Wygdor, all of whom perished in the Holocaust.
May their souls rest in eternal peace.

In honor of my dear daughters, Helen and Grace,
and my wonderful grandchildren: David, Stephen,
Daniel, Maura, and Benjamin. May they enjoy
long, peaceful lives with the ones they love.

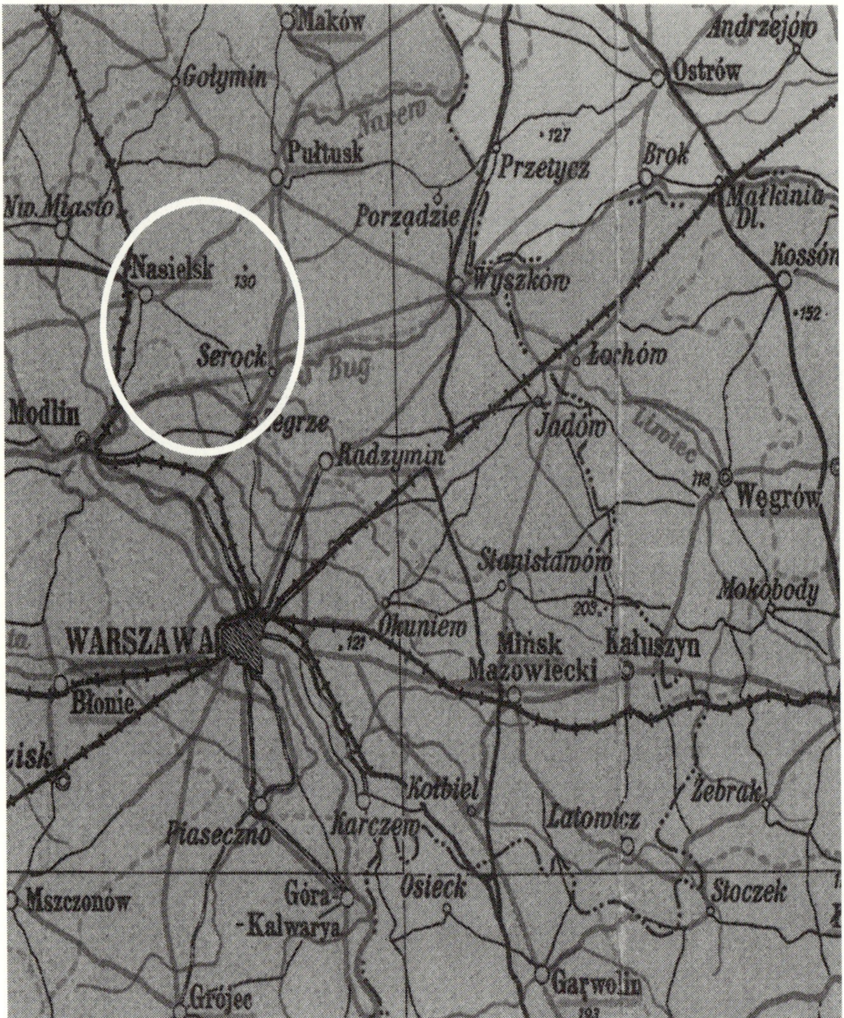
Maków
Gołymin
Andrzejów
Ostrów
Narew
Pułtusk
Przetycz
Brok
Nw. Miasto
Porządzie
Małkinia
Dl.
Kossów
Nasielsk
130
Wyszków
152
Serock
Bug
Łochów
Modlin
Zegrze
Radzymin
Jadów
Liwiec
118
Węgrów
Stanisławów
Mokobody
203
WARSZAWA
121
Okuniew
Mińsk
Mazowiecki
Kałuszyn
Błonie
Kołbiel
Żebrak
Piaseczno
Karczew
Latowicz
Mszczonów
Góra
-Kalwarya
Osieck
Stoczek
Garwolin
193
Grójec

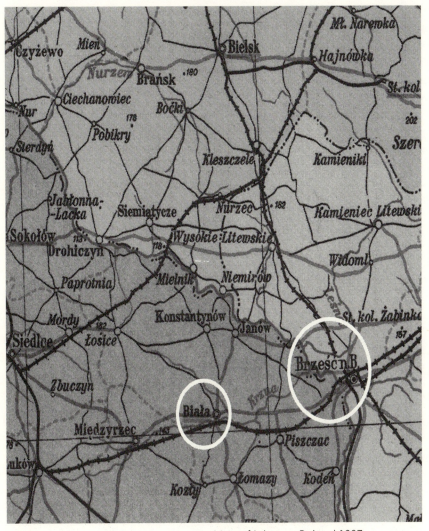

Map of Interwar Poland 1927.

I have gone by the name Sabina Mazurek," I tell the clerk at the Displaced Persons Center, "but I was born Bella Kuligowska. I am a Jew."

There, I have said it.

I have pronounced the words that I have ached to cry out for so long. All those lonely years, I longed for the chance to declare that I am not the girl I seem to be. I yearned for a true friend, someone I could trust with my enormous secret, my extraordinary burden. I yearned to take off my shield and release my pent-up feelings, my fears, and my grief.

The clerk stares at me in disbelief.

"I am a Jew," I repeat, standing firmly in front of his desk. "I am a Jew."

"I don't believe you," he says flatly. "You have no signs of being Jewish. You don't even speak Yiddish. You are a Pole. You should not be trying to get extra privileges by pretending to be a Jew."

With one hand, he motions for the next applicant to step forward, dismissing me.

I am stunned, momentarily speechless.

"You are mistaken, sir," I finally muster. "You must believe me."

I continue to protest. I speak into the air while the clerk goes on to the next person in line. Pestered sufficiently, the clerk finally returns his attention to me. He puts down his pen, walks over to the head of the displaced persons' camp, a man who listens, nods, and comes over to me with accusing eyes and a frown. Worse than not believing that I am Jewish, he seems to think I might be a spy.

The director quizzes me on the Jewish blessings.

"*Baruch atah…*" I recite the blessing over bread and the one for eating potatoes.

"Now tell me what you say when you see lightning and hear thunder," he instructs.

"I don't remember," I tell him pitiably. "It has been such a long time since I allowed myself to remember that I am Jewish. I've had to push my past into the deepest part of my memory, because I was terrified it might spill out and reveal my true identity."

Then, I share the story of my transformation…

PART ONE

My Childhood

I f only I could recreate the smells of my mother's kitchen on Friday evenings, *erev Shabbos*, each week. The delicious scents called to my stomach and signified the arrival of the one day of the week when business stopped and pleasure reigned. I remember the steamy chicken soup with soup nuts, or *mandlen*, the fresh-baked challah, the meat-filled *kreplach*, the noodle *kugels*, the roast, the gefilte fish, and the breaded veal chops, fried on both sides until crispy and brown. Since observant Jews cannot cook on the Sabbath, my brothers and I would carry the food for Saturday lunch down to the basement on Fridays, where it would stay cool.

After bathing and dressing in our finest clothes on Friday afternoon, my mother and I lit *Shabbos* candles while my father led my brothers to the synagogue. Then, on *Shabbos* morning, after synagogue, the men never came home alone. My father, ardently observant of *mitzvahs*, or obligations between man and his fellow man, happily fulfilled the requirements of *hachnosas orchim* by inviting guests, usually from the local yeshiva, for every Sabbath meal.

For lunch on Saturday, the main course was *cholent*, a hearty stew that cooked ever so slowly all night, from before dusk on Friday until mealtime on Saturday. My little brothers always brought the big, heavy pot to the communal oven before sundown Friday. My mother made a deluxe version of the traditional dish, with more than the usual potatoes, beans, barley, spices, and meat; she added sweet *kugel* and *kishke* made by stuffing the skin of the chicken neck, the *gorgel*. Every bite of the rich, brown stew was heaven. I can still taste it now.

On Saturday, we often walked to *shul* as a family. Our synagogue, a simple *shtiebl*, was just a few blocks away, above a nondescript courtyard. The fixtures and furnishings were made of primitive, stark wood. The revered *Aron Kodesh*, the ark of the Torah scrolls, stood as its centerpiece, and both the main sanctuary and the woman's balcony faced it. Above it hung the *ner tamid*, the eternal light. There was also another synagogue, a little bigger than ours and freestanding. I remember attending that one on national holidays, such as Constitution Day, the third of May. On these days, the Jewish and Christian children would march together until a certain point, when we would split off, and the Christian children would go to church, and we would go to synagogue.

• • •

I must confess: before the war, I was very young, took way

too much for granted, and was self-centered. I pursued a carefree life and was ever the spoiled child, the pet of the family, the only daughter in a family of many boys, so I was prized. My darling father could not begrudge his only daughter anything. When I wanted a coat made of embroidered sheepskin, he bought me one. When I asked for a silk scarf, he brought me a dozen from Warsaw. When I begged for more money to buy sweets from the store next to his shop, he came home with a whole case full of candy.

What Bella wants, Bella gets—that was the motto at home.

But I could still get in trouble. When I was very young, I loved to splash and dance in the rain. I would stand with my feet under the downspouts or frolic with friends in the gutter, which filled with massive puddles. I could be so foolish. When I was ten, my mother warned me that it was dangerous to jump in the deep water of the gutters because I could not see what might be at the bottom.

On the eve of our final day of school one year, I pranced merrily home through the puddles singing the "School Year Ends" song.

With a song,
We the classmates part
Life quickly floats away
Like a surge,
Time is running its course.
In a year, in an hour,
In a moment,
Each of us will part
And we go our own way.

As I finished the song, my foot landed on a broken bottle, the jagged glass cutting right through my shoe and tearing into my flesh. The pain didn't bother me as much as the fear of what my mother would say.

I raced home, furtively bandaged my foot with a towel, and went to bed early. The next day, when it was time to get up for school, I tried to convince my mother that I was sick.

"You have to go, Bella," she said. "It's the last day. Besides, you don't look sick."

She pulled off my blanket and discovered the bloody mess: sheets, towels, and all. Shaking her head in quiet rebuke, she called for the doctor, who bandaged my foot properly. I limped to school while my mother changed my bed linens.

I imagined her in my head saying over and over, "I warned you."

I should tell of my family. We are from Serock, Poland, a little town about forty kilometers north of Warsaw, between Warsaw and Pultusk. I was born July 7, 1925, and I was the fourth child with three older brothers: Abraham, the oldest; Israel; then Benjamin. After me, there were two more boys, Joseph and then Wygdor. I can recall how we scrubbed the apartment when preparing for Wygdor's birth. The water was boiling on the stove, and clean sheets and towels were spread out everywhere.

When the midwife arrived, everyone left the house. When we came back, I had a brand-new baby brother. He was wrapped in clean, white sheets so tightly from head to toe that he could not move his arms and legs. He looked like a little Egyptian mummy.

Joseph and Wygdor were together so much it was hard to tell which one was the older. But they did not look at all alike. Wygdor resembled my father, with the same Gentile-like features that Benjamin and I showed. Of all my older

The Kuligowski family taken in Serock, 1937.
LEFT TO RIGHT: Back Row: Benjamin, Abraham, Israel;
Seated: Bezalel and Chaya;
Front Row: Wygdor, Bella, Joseph

brothers, it was Benjamin whom I most resembled, with our similar Kosciuszko pug nose. Joseph resembled my mother and Israel; they had dark hair and dark eyes and looked much more Jewish than the rest of us.

My mother had been a seamstress when she was younger and had operated her own dressmaking business. Her work was what brought my parents together; when my mother's sewing machine needed repair, she called on the town's best young mechanic. My father was twenty-two years old then, and his shop was the size of a shed. They fell in love and were married when she was nineteen.

Mama stopped working before the wedding because my father did not want his wife serving others. He did not like finding her on the floor, trying to make a straight hem on some stranger's dress, and clothes making back then was primitive. She did not own any modern technology, just an early model sewing machine. But she had a real talent and continued to sew clothing for herself and her growing family; she sewed all my dresses and shirts and also underwear for my father and brothers. She would work by the light of a small electrical lamp that Abraham installed above her sewing machine. She was so dedicated to her family. My mother would be up sewing early each morning, before anyone else, but the moment any of us began to stir, she would put aside her work and turn her attention to us.

Though my mother was not supposed to work, she had learned about fixing bicycles just by watching our father. I remember once a man came to the shop after hours with a flat tire. He assumed he was out of luck when he found none of the men in our family home. My mother, however, did the job herself. I was as astonished as the customer to see my mother expertly remove the bad tire from the bicycle, separate the inner tube, pump air into it, locate the leak, patch it, and place it in water for a final test. My mother refused to accept money; the customer's gratitude and respect were ample compensation for her.

My father's talents enabled him to create a flourishing business that allowed our family to stay together. Most other families were not able to afford that luxury, and one or more members usually traveled far away to earn a living. For example, one of my mother's two brothers was a hatmaker in Nasielsk. They were not very well off financially, and I remember sleeping on a straw bed in their dark apartment when we visited them. My uncle could not find work there for his daughter, so my father opened a notions store for my cousin in Serock. I used to sit at the store, watching my cousin practice her craft.

There were only two reasons for trade-related travel in my family: one was that my father's shop had become so successful that he had opened a second one in a nearby town, and the other was that parts and supplies had to be ordered in Warsaw and then shipped to Serock by train.

My father's forty-kilometer excursions to Warsaw came several times a week. Every time he returned, he brought salami, corned beef, bologna, and other meats, along with rolls and sweet rolls. During vacations from school, I occasionally had the privilege of going with him on the hour-long horse-and-carriage ride. We would walk through the cobblestone streets of Warsaw's Jewish section, smelling the variety of foods cooking in every building. My father would treat me to a bowl of hot chicken soup with noodles for lunch between business meetings.

Everyone in my family was mechanically inclined and helped where we could. My eldest brother, Abraham, had convinced my father to go into semiretirement before the war. Abraham, whom we called "Avrum," held the family together in those days, running the shop and assigning us tasks. His own specialty was decorative paint on the bicycles. He was very artistic as well as being a budding engineer. He built the oven for firing the bicycles and also built a camera from scratch. I was his favorite photographic subject. He enlarged one picture and it hung in our kitchen: a portrait of me in a blouse and a straw hat with multicolored flowers on it.

Abraham was drafted into the Polish army in 1938, when he was twenty-one. Due to his tall, slim, handsome physique, he was recruited by the horse artillery division, a prestigious assignment. Within a short while, he became known for his mechanical skills and gained the respect of his superiors. Over the course of his military service, Abraham survived five horses being shot dead under him. In August 1939, his division rode past Serock on its way from Warsaw, to the front, to fight the Germans. Abraham left his belongings with his officer, although doing so was against protocol, and came home to say good-bye. My mother fainted on the spot.

When Abraham was drafted, my second brother, Israel, whom we called "Srulek," took on much of the responsibility for the shop, and he expanded the business by introducing new types of merchandise. Had Israel lived, he certainly would have made a career in fashion. He was the one who taught me to put my stockings on straight. *See, feel the seam with your middle finger, starting at the heel. Now go up your leg straight as you can. See?* It was Israel who had styled my mother's hair on Fridays in honor of the Sabbath. He would wash her hair like a professional and pin it up with the special hairpiece she had made to cover her own hair. This was a compromise she had struck with my father, who was less stringent religiously than she was. She had wanted to cover all her hair with a wig and a scarf, as the Orthodox Jews do and as her mother did before her.

Israel was such a perfectionist about clothes. One time he took his girlfriend and me to see a movie and bought us all candy. When the candy spilled on his pants, he was too upset to enjoy the rest of the movie. Israel was also the most generous person I have ever known. Before the war, he bought me gifts—of fine lingerie—even more often than Abraham, who showered me with cosmetics.

Unfortunately, Israel was frail. He never served in the military due to his chronic illness, a weakness of heart that left him struggling for breath most of his life. My parents had taken him to a doctor in Warsaw before the war, but they did not find a cure.

Benjamin, called "Beenam," the brother born just before me, managed my father's second shop, which was located in the neighboring town of Zegze. When he came home, he would bring me jewelry from Zegze, and once he even brought me a fancy manicure set. It was Benjamin who escorted me to dances and always returned me home by nine o'clock, my father's strict curfew for his only daughter. Any dance he went to, Benjamin had to take me, and he would dance with me too. I was the little princess of the family. My brothers would do anything for me—with the exception of my schoolwork.

All my brothers were good students, but my brother, Joseph, outshone them all. Had the war not started, Joseph, whom we called "Yossel," would have been the first of all the brothers to go to trade school or to high school. Who knows what he might have become?

During vacations from school, my job was applying the background paint to the bicycle frames. I remember one hot summer morning, I tried to sneak away to the river before finishing my day's work. I was caught by my father, who taught me a stern lesson in responsibility.

I was also the family runner, meaning I collected stock from the storage rooms in the yard and brought them into the shop, a job that fit my personality perfectly. In the days of my carefree youth, I simply never stopped moving. I cannot think of a single time when I sat through a whole meal with my family except during the holiday of *Sukkos*, when the canopy of the sky was visible through the branches that covered our little holiday booth and the lively decorations kept me sufficiently distracted.

Occasionally I was allowed to sell parts to customers when the store was busy. On Friday afternoons, I rode my bicycle through the woods, about half a mile, to bring Benjamin food for the Sabbath. Benjamin would stay near the Zegze shop six days a week, even though he himself did not work on the Sabbath, because there were non-Jewish workers who kept the business open on Saturday.

All of my brothers helped my parents discipline me. The two younger ones delighted in spying on me and then telling our parents when I went somewhere or did something without permission. And I did both. One time when we were all little, I had let a girl take a ride on a bicycle from my father's shop. It had been against the rules, but I had wanted to be generous with this poor blacksmith's daughter. Joseph and Wygdor chased her until she fell down and broke her leg. My parents paid the doctor's bill and then provided her family with meals.

Then there were our grandparents. I was very close to my grandmother, Rivka, my mother's mother, who was born around 1880, near the Russian border and lived in Serock. I will cherish forever the closeness and security I felt when I was with her. She taught me how to work with different colors of beads. We made capes, collars, bracelets, and necklaces, and I wore each piece with great pride. My grandmother used to spend most of *Shabbos* at our home. If, by chance, she could not come over, I would bring the entire Sabbath meal to her house. Often when I visited her on Saturday afternoons, I would find her sitting out in front of her house, holding a *siddur*. While her lips moved, I am not sure if she actually knew how to read the prayer book. And I will never know.

Her husband, my grandfather Herschl, I only recall a bit, and my memories of him are overshadowed by his terrible death.

It was one cloudy, chilly autumn morning during my elementary school years. I remember that the sun was just pushing through the clouds, showing the promise of a lovely day. My grandfather was walking on the side of the road on his way home from a nearby village. There was no public transportation in our town; we got everywhere by walking or using a horse-drawn carriage. Cars were a rare sighting. But on that particular day, a car did pass through our town, just at the time when my grandfather was out.

The car hit him, killing my beloved grandfather instantly. His body was found hours later in the ditch beside the road. There was no police investigation; the car and driver were long gone.

I do not remember my grandparents on my father's side—I don't even know their names. Abraham once found a small photo of them. He took the picture to Warsaw and had it converted to a portrait, which he hung on the wall. In the picture, my grandmother was young and pretty, her hair combed up high and held with a ribbon or a pin. She had a dignified expression on her face, and she wore a dark outfit, and a white, ruffled high collar outlined her neck. My grandfather wore a dark suit, a white shirt buttoned up to his neck, and a Russian-style dark hat. His beard was dark and bushy, though he kept it neatly trimmed, and his face radiated kindness and pride. They looked like members of Russian royalty.

My father told me only a little about them. They were bakers and owned a shop located in a basement somewhere in town. During his childhood, my father helped with chores in the bakery and learned to make wonderful treats. Later, when I was young, he taught me how to braid a six-stick challah, how to make sweet rolls filled with raspberry jam, and how to prepare *pletzlach*, flatbread with onions. My mother would ready all the dough, and then I would spend all day every Friday creating and baking the *Shabbos* goodies. At the end of the day, I presented my family with the most wondrous array of baked goods, all made because of my father's teachings, which he learned from his parents.

I should explain about our town. Serock was a wondrous little town where everybody was a friend or a neighbor. It was home to about thirty-five hundred Jews and thirty-five hundred Poles. It was built around water, since the Narew and Bug rivers met in front of the town, crashing into each other like wild rams from opposite direction. They joined and spiraled into a wild tumbling, like water in a boiling kettle. The current was so violent that no one could swim across it. Two teenagers were once caught in those waters and drowned, their bodies never recovered. Eventually the different shades of greenish and bluish waters made peace and blended into the Wisla river seven kilometers away. There were plenty of places where we could either swim or row a boat across the waters, since they were not wide, and on the other side lay miles of beautiful open prairie.

The church of Serock was perched precariously at the very top of the mountain. Its steeple was visible from the riverbank and from the lowest valley of the town. It was quite a sight to behold.

Everyone seemed to know me in Serock, and when I was old enough to be on my own, I would go around and make visits. I might see a neighbor to play with their baby. I would often drop in at my cousin's notions shop to admire the lovely ribbons and bows that she sold, fingering the needles and thimbles.

When there was no school, I would go to a bakery owned by the parents of one of my friends. They made little loaves of pumpernickel and would offer them to me as soon as they were cool enough. There is nothing as succulent as freshly baked Polish bread. Then, if I felt like it, I would stop at a fruit store and admire their stock. Life was lighthearted fun, and I was at my happiest when I was with my family.

I remember the first place that I called home: our apartment on Kosciuszko Street. Our rooms were located up a steep and squeaky staircase and down a long, second-floor hallway that was so dark one had to feel their way to the door. The apartment itself was large, clean, and cozy. Big windows in the living room faced the street, and in the summer, the windows were kept open, in order to have enough fresh air. During the winter, in addition to the apartment's heater, the sun's rays shining in kept us warm.

We lived in this apartment for a few years. Harry and Fay Wenger lived next door to us, only a thin wall separating our apartments. Their youngest son, Morris, was the same age as me. I remember starting school with him, at seven years old. We were in the same homeroom until we graduated. He knew how to embroider, crochet, and mend better by far than some of the girls in the class. But then, Morris was far more talented than most everyone in our class, girl or boy.

The square, cement courtyard behind the building was my playground. The space was ringed by garden apartments, which were home to some of our neighbors, and my father's tiny shop was in a corner. I remember it vividly; it was small, the size of a shed, and crowded with all kinds of wonderful junk.

We were fortunate; even in that first apartment, we slept on straw mattresses and kept linens meticulously clean. The washing process took two or three days. The linens were washed by hand, bleached, blued, and starched. Then they were taken to the mangle, where every last wrinkle was removed from the sheets and pillowcases, the hand towels with little designs embroidered on them, the tablecloths, and napkins. Only then were the linens worthy of being put back on the straw mattresses.

The mangle was used by everyone in Serock. Located in the market square, it was housed in one vast, unlit room, which could therefore be used only during the daylight hours. I often accompanied my mother to the mangle along with some of my brothers. One person had to put the linens through the front of the mangle, stretching the fabric and sprinkling it with water. A second person, generally the strongest among us, would hand crank the huge contraption. A third person was needed to grab the linens as they came out the back and make sure they fell straight, so that no creases would form. Then two people would jointly fold the clean laundry, as neatly as professional cleaners.

In a few short years, my father's business had grown in popularity. He was known as a man who could fix most anything, and in addition, Father expanded his business into selling and renting bicycles. Eventually, the shop in the courtyard became too small, and we had to move to a better, larger location. I was still young so I do not remember much of the move. But I remember that I insisted on moving to the new location while riding on my bicycle. My older brothers indulged me, taking turns pushing me up the steep hill to our new home.

Our second family home was on Warsaw Street, the main thoroughfare where there were many stores. My father's shop, which was long and narrow, was up a few stairs from the sidewalk. Our apartment was behind the shop and had just two rooms. To the left of our building, there lived a female dentist. And to the right, on the same side of the street, there was a grocery store. The young couple who owned the grocery store had a little girl. Farther up the street, there was a bakery. It was not uncommon for families to live and work in the same location.

Behind our house were a police station and a jailhouse. The jailhouse was a simple shed that locked from the outside with a hook, which says something about the extent of crime in our community. Sometimes the door to the jail was left open, and I would wander nearby exploring, but I was always too scared to go inside.

—

My family moved to our third and last home in the mid 1930s. It was a few blocks farther than the last one, closer to the outskirts of town. This house was quite different from the one we moved out of. It was far larger and far more comfortable than our earlier homes.

The shop was on the ground level at the front, with the family living space in back. The kitchen was bright and large, and there was a window facing the backyard and a door leading to the yard a few steps to the right. In the middle of the kitchen stood a stove with two burners that we used for cooking all year-round. In the winter, it kept us warm as we gathered to cook and eat our meals. To the left of the kitchen, in a corner alcove, stood a double bed where two of my brothers slept. That bed, covered with a blue bedspread, was always immaculate. Along the same wall were built-in cabinets with drawers in which we kept our dishes and silverware and stored food. A butcher block in the kitchen was the place where the bread and rolls were stored and cut. On the other side of the back door, facing the window, stood the kitchen table, and to one side was Abraham's portrait of me, hanging on the wall.

A door opened to the dining room. I loved that room. There were red runners on the wood floors surrounding a large table that was covered with a burgundy velvet tablecloth. On the windows there were lovely curtains. The walls were a testament to our family with pictures of my parents, my brothers, my grandparents, my aunts, and uncles all crowding together, fighting for space. The bedroom was decorated with green velvet curtains and a green velvet bedspread.

Our neighbors to the right, the Laska family, were separated from us only by a thin wall. They had a tiny grocery store with meager stock. I do not remember how large the family was, but I remember their daughter, Bella Laska, well. She was a bit older than me, and I loved to be around her. We used to go hiking, walking to the bank of the river, or exploring the Napoleon Mountains and pick violets and lilies. Sometimes she would help my mother prepare Sabbath meals, or we would just sit in front her parents' store and chat. I remember watching in admiration while she brushed her long, gleaming hair in the sun.

To the left of our house was the candy store, a treasure of anticipation for me when I was younger, and I visited it often. Across the street was the *Kino*, or movie house, more shops, and a bus stop. On school days, during recess, I would run down the hill to the brook, which we called the *zdui*, that flowed down from the mountain above. The water seller filled his barrels there every day; this is where the people of Serock collected their drinking and cooking water.

My mother once showed me stacks of beautifully embroidered towels, linens, sheets, and tablecloths, all monogrammed with my initials. She said this was just the beginning of the dowry she would give me when I wed. It was the custom of our people to accumulate such dowries, and my mother spared no effort or expense for mine. I was the only daughter of a middle-class family. I was too young to appreciate what she was showing me then; only in retrospect do I recognize her devotion to my future happiness.

—

I was famous for my love of sweets, candy, and pastries. Wednesdays and Fridays were market days, and I would go to the *rynek*, or market square, early in the morning and make my way through the throngs of housewives busily selecting their eggs, fruits, vegetables, and fish. I did not like the smells of the goats, pigs, horses, and cows for sale—too heavy, too pungent, too full of manure—but my nose was trained to trace the scent of the baked goods. I was always among the first to find the man who traveled back and forth by bus bringing freshly baked bismarks and sweet rolls from Warsaw.

On school days, my mother gave me a kaiser roll and lunch money. Inevitably I would spend the money at a shop on the way to school, not on lunch foods, but on chocolate and halvah. At lunchtime, my grandmother Rivka, who lived near the school, would meet me at the door with hot soup and meat. Embarrassed to eat such a luxurious meal in front of my classmates, I would lead her to the darkest corner under the stairs.

• • •

Romualda Trauguta, our newly built and enormous school, had been named after a hero of Poland's failed uprising against Russia in the 1880s. It was located on the outskirts of our little town, where the residential and commercial area measured only about one and a half miles long by one and a half miles wide. My school friends and I had fun together, playing and hiking. We romped in the schoolyard, ran around the huge gymnasium, and walked through the wide, bright hallways. Most of the children in my class were

Bella's class photo from Romualda Trauguta School, Serock, Poland, 1938. She is pictured in the 3rd row from the bottom, 3rd from the left with a white tie. Her friend Morris Wenger is pictured 2nd row from the top, first on the right.

Jewish, but a few Poles were transferred in because they had been picked on. They were all equally my friends. Polish or Jewish—it made no difference to me.

The school's setting at the edge of town made a deeper impression on me than any class. Forests, brooks, hills, and valleys surrounded the school. It looked like a magnificent work of art that changed with the every season.

In the fall, as we began our studies, nature began to prepare for the coming winter. Yellow leaves fell gently from the trees, forming a blanket on the ground, protecting the roots against the bitter cold to come.

In the winter months, it was still dark when I left for school in the morning. Often the wind howled, chasing snow into my path. I waded through knee-deep drifts as soft snowflakes blew into my face, blinding me and stealing my breath. By the time I reached the school a mile away, my eyebrows and lashes were silvery white with frost, which contrasted with my red cheeks and the tip of my frozen nose. I looked forward to the end of the day in the winter, when I could take my snow skates and head to Pharmacy Street. I think I was the only girl in town with snow skates. My father had not intended to give them to me, but I used a pair from our store, and of course, they could not be sold after I had used them.

Spring returned at last with a gust of fragrant air. Our majestic rivers flowed proudly, and trees whispered gently in the surrounding forests, exchanging tales about the harsh winter months. The chirps of returning birds joined the symphony. I would listen carefully, trying to discern nature's secrets as I rode my bicycle or hopped from one flowerbed to another on the mile-long walk to school.

Looking back, I never witnessed a more wondrous time than those spring days, when the grass turned green, wildflowers bloomed, and the whole earth suddenly seemed to blossom, releasing its magical scent. It felt like paradise, the Garden of Eden of the twentieth century.

As the weather grew warmer, we all knew that vacation was drawing near. The sun's glow reached the very core of my being. I was afraid of the caterpillars that suddenly filled the schoolyard. The boys knew this and would chase me around with them, sending me off shrieking. Bees and caterpillars aside, I loved the gorgeous summer days. I sang a song, the "Song of the Beautiful Summers," that captured the beauty of the season.

Down in the valley by the river
Sat a beautiful maiden
Lovely as a red rose.
She sat there in the valley
By the river, in the tall grasses,
Picking the wildflowers that grew all around her.
She wove them into wreaths
And threw them into the river one by one,
The huge waves picking them up and
smoothly carrying them on their backs
To a distant, mysterious destination.

With so many adventures to be had outside of school, I resented the early days of my formal education. When I started school at the age of seven, my parents had to drag me there every day. They might have taken pity on me and let me stay home, but school was required by law. My early work, unlike my brothers', did not shine. I had so little motivation that I barely managed to be promoted from class to class.

In the upper grades, I started to realize that education and knowledge would open doors for me. I shot quickly to the top of my class and completed all seven years of public school that were available in Serock. This relatively rare accomplishment, however, was not enough for me. I desperately wanted to attend high school. Except there wasn't one in our town, and my parents were reluctant to send me away to live among strangers for more studies.

I was a bit sheltered. My parents had purchased a hardware store as my future dowry. Their plan was for me to manage it from the time I finished school until I married.

The store—one long, narrow, dark room—was not my destiny of choice. I envied the older girls who came home on vacation, dressed in their beautiful high school uniforms. They all looked so pretty and neat. I wanted to be smart and beautiful, like them. I wanted to learn the songs they sang, the dances they danced, the knowledge they absorbed. I wanted to live, learn, and laugh.

With tears in my eyes, I begged my parents to allow me to attend high school. "I can't live without it," I told them—at the time, I did not know how much greater my problems would become.

Finally my parents agreed. They promised to send me to high school the following year. I kissed and hugged them, bubbling with aspirations.

"You are just beginning to appreciate life and its beauty," my father said. "I hope that many more events in your life will bring you this kind of happiness."

I began to prepare for the high school entrance exams,

poring over grammar charts, vocabulary lists, and math problems. Nothing was more important to me then. I did not think twice about leaving my family in order to study. Before I got the chance to enroll, however, the war broke out and changed everything.

•   •   •

Looking back, we had wonderful lives in Serock. In 1922, before I was born, my father had left my mother and their first three children and moved to Argentina for two years. He had gone with a group of friends, with the hopes of making better money. Papa got a job doing mechanical work, and he sent money back to Mama for the family to live on. Papa's friends didn't have such success and decided to come back in 1924, and he came back with them to rejoin his family. My two younger brothers and I were born after that.

Papa had brought two little diamond earrings for Mama from Argentina. She saved them for me, but I had to give them up during the war.

Sometimes I wonder: What if he hadn't come back? What if he had sent for Mama and my older brothers? Our family might have lived in South America together. Our family might have survived.

Bella and her mother Chaya in Serock before the war.

PART TWO

The War

Nature declared September 7, 1939, a beautiful autumn day in Serock. The Germans, however, had declared war on Poland six days earlier, and they made September 7 the worst day in the history of our little town. Rumors had been flying for weeks, and the Polish government had just begun to mobilize troops, but they hadn't expected an invasion so soon. German airplanes came fast into Polish airspace and destroyed the Polish Air Force, meanwhile, the soldiers and their panzer tanks came storming across the border, overwhelming the Polish army. When the Germans attacked, hysteria broke out. The Polish people were as unprepared as their government and army.

I remember lying under a tree while the airplanes passed almost incessantly overhead. I was transfixed. Life had come to a standstill. I was too young then to understand the tragedy of war, to realize that this moment would end an entire chapter of my life—that my childhood had been abruptly cut off—and would change everything for us all. I look back now and know the memories of my early childhood were the foundation of my strength and the driving force for my survival.

On that day, the German planes simply appeared in the sky and started dropping bombs. There was such panic. I remained under that tree and watched in terror as the townspeople ran in all directions, searching out a safe place to hide. Many ran for shelter in basements, but the German pilots flew their planes so low, they were able to see where most of the people had gone, and that's where they dropped the bombs—right on the cellars where people were cowering. Entire families were killed. The blood of children and the elderly, the healthy and the sick, the rich and the poor mingled on the streets, gushing everywhere, like water through a broken dam.

In their dazed state, people ran into the forest and the meadows, hoping the trees would obscure the pilots' views of them. A vain effort, as the planes flew low, spraying automatic ammunition in every direction.

Germany had declared war on an unarmed civilian population. The Polish military was overrun. It was all so simple, so easy.

When there was a pause in the bombardment, a confused, bewildered townspeople gathered en masse in the streets. They came from the mountains, the prairies, from the town square, from the banks of the Narew and Bug Rivers. They were looking for ways to leave, to go anywhere the Germans had not yet reached. The population of Serock was on the move. Disoriented and confused people were running, scattering in all directions.

Walking, on horses or in buggies, on bicycles—everyone was rushing away from town. My family started out on bicycles, all except my mother. She had never learned to ride a bicycle, so my brothers had mounted a seat on one side of my brother's bike for her. But we did not go very far. The rumor spread that the Germans had invaded all of Poland without a shot being fired by the Polish army. We all returned to our houses tired, dispirited, and terrified.

Not long after Germany's attack, my brother Abraham reappeared. He'd been headed for the front, and we'd seen him just weeks before, when his unit had passed near town. After the Polish army was overrun, he had escaped from a German prisoner-of-war camp when his captors had begun filtering out Jews for immediate execution. Having my beloved brother home was the only bright moment over those horrible weeks.

• • •

Quietly and without fanfare, the Germans were suddenly everywhere. Their soldiers entered our town on foot and picked the biggest houses and our brand-new school for their headquarters. Before the people realized what was happening, my part of Poland, including my beloved Serock, was part of the Third Reich. And no sooner had they settled in than directives against Jews were posted all over town.

Terror and darkness descended and held us in a stranglehold. Every day came new decrees and degradations against the Jews, and the punishment for disobedience was death. A curfew was imposed. Jews were confined to our homes after dark. Jewish businesspeople were terrified to stay in business or even walk the streets. Jews were shot on sight by soldiers, randomly, wantonly. Jews, especially the Orthodox Jews with their distinctive clothing, were stopped in the streets, beaten, shamed, and humiliated. Their beards were cut; they were stripped of their clothing, their dignity. Their flesh was torn along with their hair. Many were clubbed to death. Bodies were strewn all over town. There was no place to hide, no escape from the cruelty.

Many prominent Jewish leaders and their families disappeared. Rumor said they were locked up in Gestapo headquarters under terrible conditions, tortured until they revealed the hiding places of their valuables—jewelry, paintings, all of their wealth. Then, but only then, were they killed and their possessions stolen by the Germans. Jewish girls were afraid to go out for fear of being molested by soldiers.

A couple of days after our town was invaded, German soldiers with stretched bayonets chased many of the Jews to the market square. There, families were separated, men to one side, women and children to the other. They marched the men to the synagogue. After a few days there without any facilities—toilets, food, water—the Germans made selections. Many healthy-looking men ages seventeen to forty-five were taken away. The rest were allowed to go home.

The selected men were then marched by German soldiers all the way to East Prussia, near Königsberg for hard labor. We heard later that there was no food on the six-day march. Many of the men did not make it: the soldiers beat them and stabbed them with their bayonets.

—

There were Jews who immediately grasped the larger dangers to us all in this war and fled town. At first, it was mostly single people and those who did not have much to lose financially, since they were abandoning their homes, their possessions, everything to escape. First, they fled to larger Polish towns that had not yet been conquered by Germans, but within just a few days, we heard these towns were invaded. Next, they tried to get across the Polish borders. They fled to Russia, a country that briefly opened its borders to persecuted Jews. Many disappeared into the vast Russian landscape and were never heard from again.

My brother Benjamin was among them. In September 1939, he and his girlfriend, along with a group of their friends, left for Russia before the borders closed. He left us permanently. I missed Benjamin but was happy to know that his destiny was separate from ours. I lived in hope that he avoided everything that befell us and survived the war.

Those with businesses and property found it harder to leave. It was beyond their understanding that they might be forfeiting their lives in order to save their wealth and possessions. Such was the case with my parents. Having a store in each of two towns, which the Gentiles learned not to enter because they knew Papa was Jewish, my parents simply could not drop everything and leave. So they delayed their departure from one day to the next, denying the truth, telling themselves that Hitler could not possibly kill as many people as he said he would.

Besides, my parents' business was not the kind that could be easily packed up and taken away. It consisted of bicycles, sewing machines, hardware, and accessories of all kinds—a handyman's dream. The stock was large and

Benjamin Kuligowski
taken before the war.

heavy. They also had a paint shop, where the bicycles and machines were hand painted.

Yet we were lucky. We found ways to elude certain edicts. When the Nazis demanded that Jews relinquish all furs to them, we burned my mother's fur coat, jacket, collars, gloves, and hats. I threw my own beautiful sheepskin coat onto the fire, with sadness, yes, but with righteous defiance.

My parents kept the stores open despite the orders that Jews were not to conduct business. Kuligowski was a Polish name. In fact, there had been a time years before when a Catholic priest with the same last name had come regularly to my father's shop. The priest and my father developed a warm relationship, despite their religious differences. They joked and laughed and mused about how they had come to have the same last name. It was somewhat common for Poles of any religion to take the name of the town of their birth, and there was a village called Kuligowska Wola not far away. Perhaps both families had originated there, and that's how we had a seemingly conventional Polish surname that matched that of a Polish priest.

In addition, my brothers and I did not look excessively Jewish, so the Germans just assumed we were Poles. How many times did the German soldiers come in to have their equipment repaired? One of them actually brought me a big, red apple. Certainly he would never have done so had he suspected our true situation.

One of our good customers and a friend of my parents' was a *volksdeutsch*, or ethnic German. When the Germans conquered Poland, he was recruited to work for the Gestapo. He used to come in and warn my father to liquidate our assets and leave Poland because he knew the

Germans' secrets. He told my father that the Germans were planning to "evacuate" all the Jews right after Serock became part of the Reich. At the time, I had no knowledge of those secret conversations. My father told us about them later, after our family had been evacuated to the ghetto.

Most people around me didn't believe that the future could be as bad as some had predicted. How would it be possible to kill a whole people? How would it be possible to destroy a whole culture?

So great was the belief that such drastic actions simply could not happen, that some miracle would prevent it, that most of the Jews we knew simply did not prepare. They were paralyzed. Finally, word spread that the Germans were going to relocate all of us. My parents planned to dig holes in the stockroom and bury all their valuables. They hadn't completed this task when the Germans finally came for us, when they came for every last one of us.

Within weeks of the invasion, our little town of Serock became *Judenrein*, cleaned of Jews.

It happened in the middle of the night, in November of 1939. There was a sudden commotion: loud noises, shots in the streets, and people running around wildly. The next moment, we heard banging on our front and back doors simultaneously. The German soldiers were yelling for us to open up immediately. The next thing we knew, the SS men were inside our home with big rifles, ordering us out.

"*Eins, zwei, drei!*" they counted, and we had better be out of the house; otherwise, I was certain they would have shot us on the spot. We were still half-asleep, nearly paralyzed with fear, still in our nightclothes. We managed to grab coats and little else. Some of our neighbors did not even manage that. Barefoot and half-dressed, we followed and flowed into the stream of Jews now running to the marketplace.

On our way to the *rynek*, or market square, Abraham found his best friend, Izaak, lying in the middle of the street. Abraham wanted to stop and help him, but it was impossible. He had to think of his family first and just kept moving.

Such were the circumstances of our lives. Jews could no longer be a caring community. We were placed in the inhumane position of making impossible, heart-crushing choices. If we chose unwisely, we paid for it with our lives. So we became more selfish, more careful, more deliberate, more inverted. And we paid with our guilty consciences if we survived.

It was a chilly, moonless autumn night, darker and colder than any other I could remember. We stood in the square, waiting for the rest of the Jews to come. It took until morning for us all to be rounded up and driven like cattle to the marketplace—men, women, children, the entire Jewish population of Serock.

There was no train in Serock, so once we were all together, we were lined up and marched through the town under the blows of whips and threats of being shot. We were bewildered and disoriented. Children looked to parents, who could offer nothing but their own fear.

The Poles of our town were lined up on the sidewalks, watching us being driven along. They stood with folded arms, smirking, satisfied; we did not see a moment of pity on their faces for their long-standing neighbors, for people who considered them trusted friends. I got the impression they were happy to be rid of us. Perhaps they looked forward to moving into our homes, using our linens and tablecloths, taking over our bedrooms, and making theirs what had been ours.

It was astonishing to me. Why our neighbors? Why my schoolmates? Why even those whom my own papa had helped in so many ways? How could this betrayal have been so complete?

We walked all day toward the town of Nasielsk, twenty-two kilometers away. The Germans rode on horseback or on motorcycles, and we were made to keep up on foot. We marched on the right side of the road, all while the Germans cracked whips and threatened death. Many old and sick people faltered, and were shot. Others who stumbled were trampled by the horses. The dead or injured were left on the roadside. Stronger Jews tried to help the weaker ones; mothers carried their smallest children, while others clung to their skirts.

My brother Israel suffered from rheumatism, so the walk was too much for him. My other brothers and father took turns carrying him, but when their strength ran out, Israel fell to the ground. He was just about to be shot when my father managed to pick him up and carry him again.

In Nasielsk, the survivors were all crowded tightly into a synagogue. There was barely room to move. There, we waited for two days until we were driven, again on foot, to the train station, where we were packed into freight cars. Again, there was no room to move, much less to sit down. There was barely enough air entering the cars for anyone to breathe.

We still had no food or water. When the early-morning dew ran down the walls of the car, people caught the dirty, rusty drops in their hands, hoping to bathe their dry throats in anything resembling liquid. Whenever the train stopped, we screamed and yelled for water or for any kind of help, but no help came. It was so terrible, and we did not know our destination.

Some prayed; others lost their faith saying, "There is no God. If there were a God, He would not let us suffer so much."

And it was only the beginning.

• • •

We spent five more days in a cattle car with the same smothering air, the same desperation for water or food, the same lack of toilet facilities. Again, those of us who survived were lined up, weak, humiliated, and dirty. We had arrived in Biała Podlaska and were taken into the local Jewish ghetto.

The Jews in town were waiting for us. They mingled with us and helped us with food, clothing, and shelter. We were one of many trains full of people that came from yet another small Polish town. Conditions in the ghetto were horrible. It was already full beyond tolerance, with people from other places crowded into rooms barely large enough to hold two people, let alone whole families. There was no privacy for even the most simple, basic functions, and the more people who arrived, the less food, clothing, and living space there was for all of us.

I remember the tiny apartment my family shared with another family consisting of a mother and her daughter and son. Together we were eleven people: my parents; my maternal grandmother, Rivka; and my brothers Abraham, Israel, Joseph, and Wygdor; Israel's fiancée, Fela; me; and the three members of the other family.

I was close to my sister-in-law-to-be, Fela Jagoda. She had been engaged to my brother Israel when the Germans occupied Serock. Her father had been arrested but had somehow escaped, and they had left immediately for Russia, her mother's birthplace. Fela had stayed behind waiting for Israel to go with her, but before the couple had a chance to leave, the Russians closed the border. She had been forced to remain in Serock and was with us through the hard transition to Biała Podlaska. Israel and Fela were married there, in our half-apartment, with my mother's wedding ring.

It was agreed that the other family would use the little kitchen, and we took the living room. We slept on the cold, bare floor on bunks, on top of the cold fireplace and in the cold hallway. We lived under these conditions for a while, without money or any work to make a living. We depended on the food rations that were given to us by the Jewish Committee of Biała Podlaska.

It was there in Biała Podlaska that we lost my grandmother Rivka. Somehow she had survived the many kilometers of walking to Nasielsk and the terrible conditions packed into the train cars as they pushed us across Poland. She held on and bravely stayed with us all the way to the ghetto. Then, in early 1940, she died of hunger in her little corner of a bench bed she had been forced to call her own, in the one room we all shared in the tiny apartment.

—

The original Jews of Biała Podlaska still had their rights, their homes, and their possessions. For example, our neighbor across the hall was wealthy. The man dealt in leather goods before the war. These locals did not yet feel what we felt; they had not yet gone through what we had gone through. They made us, the refugees, feel inferior.

In the meantime, we struggled on, woke up each day with the hope that the war would soon be over. And somehow, life went on. We got to know people around the ghetto. I became friendly with the *volksdeutsch* woman who lived upstairs, across the hall. Our apartment building straddled the boundary of the ghetto and the rest of town, so she lived in a part of the building that wasn't officially in the ghetto. I would sneak up to talk with her or one of the other less-crowded neighbors just to get away for a while.

I also met with my friends, some newly made, some from my hometown. We often talked of freedom, freedom that we were sure would come soon, but our lives also returned to a measure of normal. We would go for walks, exchange news, even talk about boys.

"Don't look now, but in a minute, look behind you and tell me if you see that tall boy," I said to my friend Sophie.

She looked over her shoulder. "Yes," she whispered.

"Well, he's been following me everywhere," I said. "Every time I look around, he's there. Do you know who he is?"

Sophie giggled. "You could do worse. His family is from right here, and I hear they're rich. That is, they were rich, until the Germans confiscated everything and threw them into the ghetto, like us."

"Do you think he wants to meet me?"

"Oh yes," Sophie said. "I'm sure he'll find a way to introduce himself. Just wait and see."

Such girl talk seemed so out of place in retrospect. But we had to adapt to the changes in our lives and continue as best we could. For our sanity, we had to continue with what had been normal just a few months ago. I remember seeing the older teenage girls being pursued by boys, going out on dates, and hanging out in groups, just as teenagers do everywhere. They sang and they shouted like normal adolescents, as if the world still belonged to them. Each of us had to find a way to cope, to block out the knowledge of the terrible fate that lay before us—because somehow we knew. We squeezed in as much living as we could, as if we knew that any day may be our last. Perhaps it is easiest for youth. Like diamonds, youth are strong and hard, and can withstand the roughest abuse. Youth do not have a lifetime of work and memories to lose.

Many reacted to the trauma by holding to religion. This was the case in my family. The more we were persecuted, the more religious we became, as if faith would bring salvation. At times, it was our only hope. In the best way we could, we observed the Jewish holidays and rituals. It seemed to ground us. We tried to hang on to our Jewish ways of life and beliefs in the traditional way, still trusting that *Moshiach*, the Jewish Messiah, would come and save us, would bring us back to the land of our ancestors—the land of Israel.

I remember hearing as a child that after *Moshiach* came, all the Jews would die and then be resurrected in Israel. The words are still vivid in my mind, though I do not remember whether they were directed at me specifically, or if I just over-heard them at the synagogue on Saturday with my papa. I probably misunderstood what was being said, but the words helped me believe that our nation was not dying in vain. Indeed, our nation was not going to die. It gave me hope.

As we struggled to survive and maintain some semblance of normalcy in the ghetto of Biała Podlaska, the Germans continually found excuses to abuse us. And over time, the aggression and viciousness increased.

One day Joseph burst into the apartment like a wild bear. His dark eyes, filled with tears, looked black against the chalky whiteness of his skin.

"Hide! Hide, everyone!" he shrieked.

My parents tried to comfort him, but he would not stop trembling. Finally, when we were all crouched around him on the floor, he spoke more clearly.

"I just saw the Germans run into a house filled with people, shooting everyone like crazy. They shot the men, the women, the children, everyone. Then they started singing and laughing, as if they were celebrating a grand event. It's all a big joke to them. A game!" His voice grew shrill, and his eyes were pools of fear.

Another time, Wygdor raced in and told us that he'd just escaped a raid on the street.

"The Germans rounded up everyone there," he reported. "I heard they took them to the cemetery and killed them all."

"Calm down," Mama said, trying to reassure him. "Maybe it's just a rumor. It may not be as bad as it sounds."

"Don't despair," said Papa. "We must believe that we will survive."

The situation in the ghetto became more and more dangerous. There were some Jewish collaborators that would lead the Nazis to any Jews who had managed to sneak some wealth into the ghetto. These families would be taken away and never seen again. We heard rumors they were tortured until they turned over their assets.

In exchange, the Jewish collaborators enjoyed the temporary privileges of sufficient food and the promise of survival. We could always identify these individuals by their leather clothing and boots and their freedom of movement.

During the day, we struggled to stay alive. We heard the cries of children, their bellies swollen from hunger. We heard the moans of the sick. We heard the violent shouts of the SS as they marched down the streets, invading every hiding place. Each evening, gloomy darkness slowly crept across the sky and through the gates of the ghetto, enveloping us all in the death that clung to the clouds and endlessly fell upon us like rain.

I remember seeing people walking about the streets like lunatics, raging, desperate to find a way out, desperate to just save their lives. It was like drowning in quicksand; they sank deeper and deeper into hopelessness, with no one to come to their rescue, to pull them out. They were frantic and deprived, afraid of tomorrow and what it might bring yet also afraid there would be no tomorrow.

My parents and brothers tried to shelter me within the four walls of the ghetto, but I could hear the shots of the Nazi hunters as they raided buildings and murdered the unarmed inhabitants. I could see the roundups in the street each day. Bodies and human flesh were scattered all over the streets.

People were planning, thinking, looking—for anything that might lead to escape.

• • •

My father tried to get a job through the Jewish Committee, the group that took care of the refugees, but there were so many restrictions. The Germans wanted only the young and able-bodied. There were so many Jewish residents living in Biała Podlaska who needed jobs, and many had more influence with the officials. Sometimes refugees would find work because they knew people in the town.

Those who worked for the Germans outside the ghetto never got paid. They may have gotten a little more food, but never any money. Food was so scarce then that these people were happy even with this small accomplishment—a few extra bites, never more than what would feed a cat.

Abraham, being young, strong, and skilled, finally managed to get a job in a German food storehouse. Like others who worked for the Germans, he was never paid, but he did get more food. In addition, he was able to steal some bread, sugar, and flour, which he would bring home to us.

I felt compelled to help my family too, but I had few options. Only once after we arrived had there been a task I was invited to participate in. The Nazis had found out that my father was a professional bicycle mechanic, and they brought him a transport of approximately one hundred bicycles that needed assembly for their soldiers. Most of the family worked on them together. Not Mama, of course. She might have helped, but again, Papa discouraged her. With the rest of us doing the work and being useful, we thought—we hoped—perhaps our lives would be spared. It seemed as if everyone in the ghetto was watching us work in the courtyard, a rare distraction from their daily suffering.

It was my job to assemble the spokes on the wheels. It was one of the most difficult parts of the whole process, requiring great precision. I performed my task with great speed and accuracy. I was so proud to be working as a full-fledged mechanic with my older brothers. Even those watching were amazed at my ability. I was a girl!

Thank heavens we were all mechanically inclined, a blessing that brought a temporary reprieve for our family.

But it was not enough for me. I wanted to do more, and I had an idea.

—

"Mama," I whispered in the darkness the night before my first expedition. "I am going to sneak out of the ghetto at dawn. I will try to bring back some potatoes or bread, something to eat."

My mother put her bony hand on my shoulder and opened her mouth to object.

"Mama, I have to go," I insisted. "Israel is getting weaker and weaker; we are all hungry. I can do it. Everyone says I don't look Jewish. I will be able to pass as a Pole once I get outside the ghetto." I would take my yellow Star of David off my coat and just walk out.

As the first rays of light made their way through the cracks between the crowded buildings of the ghetto, I carried out my plan, a prayer playing on my lips. Everything went surprisingly smoothly. I made my way through Biała Podlaska, toward the nearby farms. I found work for the whole day in the fields in exchange for a few potatoes and a loaf of bread, which I managed to smuggle back into the ghetto for my parents. Dressed in the clothing of a typical Polish farm girl, no one recognized me as a Jew.

My mother gasped and faltered as I entered the dim apartment after curfew.

"Mama," I called, running to her. "What happened?"

My mother looked at me with such relief. "Oh, Bella! It's you! I didn't recognize you for a minute."

My father came over to me and looked me in the eyes. "Don't ever do that again." At first I thought he was scolding me for frightening my mother. "Don't ever risk your life for us again. We are your parents. We are responsible for taking care of you. You are not responsible for taking care of us."

Then I understood. They had been beside themselves with worry. For me, it had been an adventure, and a fruitful one at that. I felt as if I had been trained for this mission, as if it were a natural role in this most unnatural drama that was unfolding for my family. I bowed my head and indicated that I had heard him, but I did not promise never to sneak out again. I wanted to help and there were so few things I could do. Besides, I was now in my teens, and Papa would have expected me to work for the business if we were still at home.

Sneaking out of the ghetto that first time was more than just a means of getting food. It gave me something to do, and it had given me a taste of the freedom I craved. In the ghetto, I felt trapped, like a caged animal. I shared one room of this apartment with my parents, brothers, sister-in-law, and my grandmother, until she passed away. We had to obey curfews and stay within the walls of the ghetto at all times. No one could leave except for work purposes.

The air was fresh outside the ghetto, where corpses did not line the streets and disease did not hang in the air. The sky was brighter and there were flowers and animals. Children went to school; parents brought home supplies and cooked food in their own kitchens. Shopkeepers opened their stores in the morning and closed them at night. People went to movies and concerts. It was so normal out there. I could not let go of this wisp of freedom. It permeated my every thought.

I repeated my outings often, each time with renewed joy and success. My parents tried to warn me of the dangers I was facing, pleading with me to be careful, urging me to return before curfew, because the Germans would certainly kill me if they caught me after dark. But I could not heed them. The little freedom I got when I left the ghetto was like a balm. It helped me forget, for just a bit, the suffering and deprivation. It gave me the hope I needed to continue struggling for my own survival.

I returned from the trip out of the ghetto one day and found my mother examining a pile of strange rags.

"Avram found these flour bags." She showed me, unwilling to say "steal" in reference to anything we pilfered from the Nazis. "I am going to use this durable fabric to make a beautiful outfit. I don't have a sewing machine here, but I can do the job by hand. Then, I'll unravel what's left, so you will have yarn to knit a sweater with. It's a little coarse, but it's better than what you've been wearing."

Abraham was sitting nearby, beaming with pride.

"I can't believe you don't want me to smuggle in food, but you let Avram risk his life so that I can have new clothes!" I shouted. I was always babied by everyone and I thought it was time that I be treated as an adult. I was fifteen years old!

"We want you to look nice," Israel chimed in from his sickbed. He was pretending to read a book but was clearly listening to our conversation. "What if you meet a nice boy and go out on a date?"

What a thought in such a world!

Of course Israel, more than anyone, wanted me to look nice, as he'd always been a perfectionist when it came to clothing. And here, even from his sickbed, he was focused on my care and my future.

The trip to the ghetto had worsened Israel's infirmity, and in the terrible conditions there, without doctors or medicine, no measure of heroism could save him. His ailing heart sapped more and more of his vital energy, until all that was left was the withered shell of my formerly fastidious brother. We could do nothing for Israel but comfort him.

"*Tatteh. Tatteh*," Israel rattled incessantly one day in 1940. No one but our *Tatteh*, our papa, could provide him with the solace he needed to slip into his eternal slumber. Finally, my father came home from a day looking for work and went directly to Israel. He held his dying son in his arms, and soon we heard Israel draw his last breath.

Had Israel died in Serock, where life was normal, people probably would have felt sorry for us. His death would have been unusual and our friends and neighbors would have crowded into our home to comfort us, to bring us food, to pay their respects. In the ghetto, death was commonplace. By the time of Israel's passing, there was hardly a family that had not lost a son or daughter to Nazi violence, starvation, or disease. Our personal family tragedies—first Benjamin escaping to Russia, where we could only pray he was alive, then our grandmother dying, and now Israel— was just another thread in the fabric of the war.

One afternoon that spring, my father came home with a stranger. My mother was sewing a shirt for Papa by hand, and I was knitting a sweater from the material left over from the unraveled flour bags. Since curfew was coming, Abraham, Joseph, and Wygdor were all in the room too.

"Mr. Wisniewski, this is my daughter, Bella." My father spoke these words in Polish. Mr. Wisniewski nodded and

Israel Kuligowski
taken before the war.

looked me up and down like a customer about to make an expensive purchase.

"Bella, say something to Mr. Wisniewski," my father urged.

I was still unsure of what was happening, but I did my father's bidding. "Hello, Mr. Wisniewski," I said uncomfortably, getting up from my seat on the cold hearth of the fireplace. "How do you do?"

The man turned to my papa. "Fine. The girl looks ok, and she speaks Polish well."

"Papa?" I whispered, almost ready to cry. "What is going on?"

My father explained that Mr. Wisniewski was a forester who lived not far from the ghetto and also owned a farm. With his help, I could escape by going to work for him. Mr. Wisniewski had come to check that I looked Polish enough and that I did not have a strong Yiddish accent.

"Mr. Wisniewski will have documents made for you," my father said. "He believes you can pass as a Christian on the other side. You must try to live as they do. Be a good girl. Don't be scared, darling."

I shook with a mix of anticipation and fear. I could not imagine shedding my identity like this, becoming a Christian, practically overnight. How could anyone do that?

Then I thought of someone who had done such a transformation—Lonka, the rabbi's daughter from Serock, who had eloped with her Christian boyfriend on the eve of Yom Kippur. What a calamity it had been! The rabbi's only child. She'd converted to Christianity and ran off on the holiest night of the year, Kol Nidrei.

Suddenly, her story was inspiration.

"I will do it," I said. And I thought of a new name for myself. I would add a simple "Isa" to the start of my first name to make it sound more Polish: Isabella Kuligowska. That's who I would become while with the forester. But I promised myself and my family that I would never forget who I really was.

To escape the ghetto, I had to take leave of my family there and then, with Mr Wisniewski. *Why me?* I wanted to ask. *Why not send one of the boys?* But I knew the answer. To the world, and even to myself, I was a skinny, little nothing. But to my family, I was a young princess, full of potential. I was their top priority.

Tearfully, quietly, I bade them good-bye and prepared to embark on a lifelong journey. I can imagine now how my parents must have felt, sending their fifteen-year-old daughter away. But they didn't bother in that moment with life lessons. Anything they had not taught me throughout my childhood, they could not teach me now.

As instructed, I walked several paces behind Mr. Wisniewski until we passed through the gates of the ghetto. We made eye contact, and I pulled the yellow Star of David band off my sleeve. He led the way through the streets of Biała Podlaska. I was both terrified and anguished at leaving my family behind. As I watched my feet move automatically down the dirt path, I realized that I had started on the road of independent life, alone among strangers.

I also wondered why this gentle farmer had decided to take me in. Was he hungry for money? Had my parents paid him? Or was he one of the righteous who took Jews in? This man had taken a huge risk. He and his wife could lose their own lives if they were found out.

Mrs. Wisniewska awaited us at their farmhouse a few miles outside of town. She had work for me to start on right away. The farmhouse consisted of one large room and an entranceway that served as a storeroom. Mr. Wisniewski placed a bed and a little table in one corner of the large room and hung a curtain to separate it from the rest of the room. These were my living quarters.

The forester's livestock amounted to one cow, some chickens, and a few pigs. I was in charge of the animals and the housework. Despite my inexperience, I adjusted quickly to my new responsibilities. Back home, I had been carefree and brave, except for my one silly fear of animals. Had anyone told me that I would ever feed pigs and chickens then milk a cow and take it out to pasture, I would have laughed out loud. In the past, I would never get close to an animal voluntarily. Yet there I was, learning these tasks as quickly as I could.

An invisible thread tied me to my family. I was homesick, thinking about them all the time. How I wished I could have gone back to be with them again. Yet I was elated to be in the sunshine and out of the ghetto, where terror and death were ever present.

I performed my daily tasks as I had been taught. I milked the cows three times a day. The forester taught me to do it his way, using two fingers of each hand. Eventually, the forester bought two more cows, which naturally meant more work for me. I had to bring all three out to pasture and then back to the barn later. One day, darkness seemed to set early. I was so lost in my own thoughts that I forgot where I was. Unknowingly, I was circling the house without recognizing it in the dim light of dusk.

At long last, the cows tired of my orbit and led the way home. It was then that I realized that one of the cows was missing. I cried desperately to the forester, begging him to forgive me. My very life depended on this job, and I was terrified that he would be angered by my carelessness. I offered to go out into the night and search for it, but the forester and his wife went instead. They soon located the cow and brought it back home. I felt relief beyond description.

Normally, this change of pace would have been a great adventure for me, but with fear and danger surrounding all our lives, my bumbling at farmwork seemed more like a tragicomedy. I made many mistakes, having been sheltered for so long, but I learned quickly from my errors and was dedicated to being the perfect, indispensible employee. And what I learned on that little farm was crucial to my future.

My boss was apparently satisfied enough with my work, as I often heard him and his wife discussing the false documents they would get me to legalize my status as a Christian.

On the farm and throughout the countryside, life was *free*.

I watched other farmers at work, envying them for their self-determination. More than ever, I envied the Polish high schoolers I saw going on hikes, happy as ever, without a care in the world. I envied all those young people, similar to me in age, who ran around together seemingly unaware of the world just outside their narrow lives.

Most of all I envied the girls who had boyfriends. I was at the age when I wanted companionship, but that would have been impossible. I was too serious, too engrossed continually in matters of life and death, and too busy constructing a false identity. I spent a great deal of time reading books. Many times I tried to have an adult perspective on the situation, but it was difficult to let go of my childish, though very normal, longings, in order to appreciate the gift of survival.

I remember sitting in the meadow with my charges, the cows, dreaming of a bright future, wondering if such dreams were still possible for many weeks. Already the past was obscured by a dark cloud, and the future held even more treacherous storms. I prayed to God, asking over and over, "Why can't I be like those high schoolers? Am I not as human as they? Am I not as capable of contributing to the well-being of humanity? Don't I have the right to live? Why can't I join them and be happy and free?"

My prayers and my longings were to no avail. I could not enjoy even the company of a puppy from the farm who constantly wanted to play. I had loved a puppy once. My father had given him to me as a gift, and I was responsible for walking him every morning. But one frigid day, I let him out of the house alone because I did not want to brave the cold. The dogcatchers seized him, and no matter how hard my father and brothers tried, they could not get him back for me. At the time it was a great tragedy, perhaps the greatest I had experienced.

On the farm, I was in no mood for the puppy. I felt like the whole world was against me, even an adorable little animal. He was encroaching on my space, on my last bit of solace. My gut reaction to him was powerfully negative. Perhaps, deep down, I was afraid that, by coming so close, he would sense my Jewishness, as a hound sniffs prey. So even while thinking about a silly puppy, I had come back to thinking about my circumstances. And something had become clear to me: to survive, I would have to make sure my own Jewishness was untraceable.

What about my family in the ghetto? I thought about them every day, praying for their welfare. How could I live without them? Every time Mr. Wisniewski went to town, I wrote a little letter to my family in Polish and sent it with him. When he returned, he would bring one back from them. Thus we communicated frequently, and I was reassured.

• • •

In the fall of 1940, the letters stopped. I continued to send my own missives faithfully, but the forester came home empty-handed time after time. My fears doubled and redoubled as the days passed. I begged Mr. Wisniewski for information. Had he talked to my family? Seen them? He assured me that he had, but they had not given him a letter for me.

I wanted to believe him. I knew things were bad in the

ghetto but had no idea how bad things might have gotten after I left. Eventually, I could not ignore my foreboding. I decided to write to Abraham in Yiddish, asking that he reply in Yiddish. I suspected that Mr. Wisniewski was receiving letters written in Polish but did not deliver them to be because the contents were too worrisome. "Have *rachmonus* (pity) on me," I wrote to my brother. "Please, let me know how everything is at home."

That very day, Mr. Wisniewski brought me a letter. In it, my brother asked that I return home immediately. He said that he had secured a new job for me outside of the ghetto. "You are young and strong," he wrote. "While you are working, you will not be harmed."

I told the forester that I intended to leave.

"You must be mad! You must not do such a foolish thing. It is far too dangerous. You're just getting acquainted with the work here. We like you; you are learning well. Stay! Your life can be spared!" he pleaded with me.

On one hand, I was too homesick and desperate to heed his warnings, too convinced that my family really needed me. On the other, I was fearful of being persuaded by his arguments. Perhaps in the recesses of my mind, I drowned out the thought that I might be making a major mistake. I left without saying good-bye.

This decision irrevocably changed my life for the rest of the war.

A pain shot through me as I walked into the empty apartment—sometimes, we just know things. My parents were gone, and I already knew it was forever. There was an eerie quiet, a sense that something terrible had happened. My hands became cold, and I could not stop walking pacing, daring the silence with the sound of my footsteps. Toward dark, Abraham came home.

"Bella!" he cried. He gathered me around the waist and held me close, hugging me as if I were a life vest in a stormy sea.

"Avrum." I said when the greetings were done. "Tell me what has happened here while I was away. Please, Avrum. I must know."

He saw how scared I was and his resolve to spare me the truth melted. "Mama and Papa were taken away." His voice was barely audible. "They took Wygdor with them. Wygdor cried and carried on; he wanted to stay here with us. But Mama and Papa would not leave without at least one of us. They still believed they could take care of us. We will never see them again."

Abraham's voice trailed off. He did not want to tell me any more details, but it did not take long for me to figure it out. At the time my parents were taken away, they were unaware of their destination. Innocent people were tricked into surrendering their lives with a promise of work elsewhere. The situation was so desperate in the ghetto that it was hard to imagine it could get any worse. The Nazis lured their victims with promises of better conditions, and for a while, Jews fell into their trap like hungry mice scrambling for a nibble of cheese.

My parents and others like them—the older, the feeble, and the very young—had been instructed to bring all of their valuables and a towel, and were given a loaf of bread apiece. They were told that family members who were already working, the young and strong among us, would join them when their jobs were completed. They didn't know their destination anymore than I did, and I will be tormented forever by thoughts of their nightmarish destiny.

My Dearest Tatteleh,

If you were here today, I would love you even more than when I was growing up. I adored you so. Your love for me showed on your face. It radiated like a sunbeam from the core of your being when I was in your presence, warming me even on the coldest of days. You never let me forget that I was your only little girl, the princess, among your five treasured sons. You made me feel like a rare gift that had been granted to you.

*You became the patriarch of the Kuligowski clan,
your pride and joy. I don't remember ever seeing you
angry at any of us. You raised us and disciplined all
of us with love and an iron fist, without ever laying
a hand on any of us. We all loved you and respected
you unconditionally. You were our pillar of support,
the source of our strength, and our role model.*

I threw myself onto the low straw bed and sobbed.
How I needed my parents. I had so much to share with
them. I needed to see them, talk with them, hear their
voices, feel their gentle caresses. Our family shrunk and
our tragedy grew. Benjamin, Grandmother Rivka, Israel,
and now Papa, Mama, and Wygdor.

I felt so painfully lonely that I did not think I could
continue living. There is an instant in all of us when despair
becomes a defining possibility. We either sink or we move
forward. Slowly, I realized that my lungs were filled with
air, that my heart was still beating, that I was alive. I would
have to go on. I would have to grow strong.

*I don't have to live anymore. I just have to exist. I have to
survive for the sake of my loved ones.*

With Abraham's help, I was introduced to my new job.
I was young, I was strong, and I was useful. I left the ghetto
early each morning with a group of older women. We
worked on improving the roads until late in the evening. I
pushed wheelbarrows full of gravel; the work was painfully
exhausting, but I knew it was all that was keeping the Nazis
from putting me on a transport. My great consolation and
the source of my strength was the fact that I could see my

two brothers, Abraham and Joseph, and my sister-in-law, Fela, every night.

• • •

It seems implausible, but conditions worsened, and then we heard rumors that the ghetto would be "liquidated." One fall day in 1940, my brothers did not return from work. Abraham risked his life to sneak back into the ghetto that night and warn Fela and me of the Nazis' plans. He and Joseph were being held outside the ghetto because they would continue their work here while the rest of us were deported. Abraham advised Fela and me to gather all our possessions in suitcases and be prepared for transportation to a different ghetto.

I noticed tears on Abraham's face. How guilty he must have felt for asking me to return from the farm! He knew he might be responsible for my death. Before he left, I begged him to be careful. If the Nazis caught him leaving the ghetto to return to his job, he would be captured and shot.

That was the last time I saw my eldest brother, Abraham.

Fela and I hastily prepared for the arrival of the SS, who were on their way to chase us out. They came even sooner than we expected, banging on doors and demanding entrance. We grabbed our suitcases and ran out. We were all gathered in the town square, where farmers' horses and wagons were waiting to transport us to Brześć, a town about forty kilometers from Biała Podlaska. We were driven under heavy guard. Those who tried to escape were shot in the back, their legs still moving as they tried to run.

Riding on the wagon with my sister-in-law, I considered my chances. Having sampled the sweet semi-freedom of life on the farm, I could not resign myself to going quietly to a bitter death. I knew that I would have to think and act fast—time was short and we were being guarded more and more closely as we proceeded.

While we were traveling, the SS walked alongside the prisoners, holding their helmets out for our valuables. I had a gold watch that Benjamin had given me when I turned fourteen, my last birthday before the German invasion. I also had diamond earrings that I had never even worn, the ones my father brought home from Argentina for my mother. With a mixture of despair and disdain, I threw them into a helmet. They were all I had except for a few rags that were left in my suitcase. If I were to escape, I would leave those behind as well.

When I mentioned the idea of escaping, Fela became very frightened and advised me not to try. We had seen what had happened to the others. I chose not to listen to her and prepared myself for my escape, figuring, calculating. I crept from one moving wagon to another, searching for the least-guarded position.

A Jewish proverb says that one who is mistaken for dead will live long. My hope for survival was renewed by that belief during that trip from Biała Podlaska to Brześć.

Not having found a safe escape route, I made my way back to the wagon where Fela was riding. She looked as shocked as if she'd seen me rise from the dead. She explained that she'd seen a woman dressed in an outfit very much like the one I was wearing—the pants my mother had made for me from the flour sacks—try to escape and get shot. She had already begun to mourn for me.

• • •

A short while after I got back to Fela's wagon, we arrived at the ghetto of Brześć. There, I met new people and saw many familiar faces from Biała Podlaska. We were the workers: young, pretty girls and strong, handsome men.

The ghetto in Brześć was terrifying. Every day, just for sport, the Germans randomly singled out a house for immediate liquidation. They would simply storm the house and kill everyone inside. Sometimes they would entertain themselves with acts of unbelievable barbarism: tearing out the hairs of the beards of grown men, poking out their eyes; smashing little babies against a wall, tearing them in half.

I refused to give up. As long as I was alive, I would look for a way out. I wandered along the barbed-wire fences of the ghetto, hoping for a hole through which to crawl. I asked Fela to join me even though she looked more Jewish than I did. I now admit that she would never have passed as Polish, and neither of us would have survived. I was willing to risk my life in trying, but she was not willing to face what she considered a certain death.

"Don't do it, Bella," she begged. "Stay here with me. Even if you do find a way, they'll shoot you the moment you get out."

Staying in the ghetto was more deadly, as far as I was concerned. I must leave immediately, at any price. I did not find a hole through which to escape, but after making inquiries, I devised a different plan. I found out that a group of Jewish men was driven out of the ghetto in a truck every morning to work on the roads. I hoped to slip in among them and get off the truck outside the gate.

In preparation, I found someone who was willing to accept my suitcase and all of its contents in exchange for a babushka and a basket, like the ones used by Polish peasants to carry eggs and butter to the market. I saved only a change of underwear, which I put into the basket and then covered it with a white handkerchief. Early the next morning, I put on my coat—a valuable resource for my survival—a wide skirt, the babushka, and slipped the basket onto my arm. I was in the uniform of a young Polish peasant girl. Quickly and quietly, I made my way to where the workers were to be loaded onto the truck, and I waited for the moment of truth.

I jumped on just after the doors were opened, and I had cowered in the darkest corner of the covered truck as the Jewish workers climbed aboard. The truck started pulling through the gate of the Brześć ghetto—so far, I had gone unnoticed. I held my breath as I heard the gate swing shut behind us. Now all that was left was to escape the group.

When the truck stopped at the work site, I stepped out with the others into the cold air. Without a backward glance, I tried to look nonchalant as I walked along the road, away from the laborers, as if I had every right to do so.

The Jewish foreman called me back and threatened to expose me. Perhaps he thought he could extort money from me.

"Don't bother me, you lousy Jew," I said defiantly, with a presence of mind and quick thinking I didn't know I had in me. I turned my back to him and quickened my pace, my heart racing. What would he do? Would he call me back again? Would I be shot in the back? Would he report me to a German guard?

I do not know whether he was fooled into thinking that I was not Jewish or whether he took pity on me. Either way, he did not bother me, and I was on my way. I didn't know where to go, nor did I take another living soul with me. I had not said farewell to my sister-in-law, since I was not sure I would succeed in escaping and did not want to worry her needlessly. The important thing was that, in that moment, I was free.

And it was time for a new identity. I wanted to distance myself from my real name, Kuligowska, and take a name that was unequivocally Christian, so I decided to use my former employers' last name. I became Stefa Wisniewska.

I walked until I came to a small farming community. I approached a small farmhouse and knocked on the door. A woman answered the door and asked what I wanted. Her husband approached as I began to speak.

"Could you use a worker here?" I said, answering a question with a question. "I will work for you in exchange for room and board. I come from a farming family and know the work." I was fabricating quickly. "We were all evacuated from the part of Poland where I lived, and I was separated from my family and friends. I have been wandering from town to town in search of them, and I want to continue, but I can't because I have nothing left. I need work. I need a place to stay and a little bit to eat."

The family, the Jablonskis, bought my story. They knew that there were Poles who had been evacuated and separated from loved ones. I looked, spoke, and acted Polish, and they needed some help on the farm. They were very poor and were glad to find a worker who did not demand a wage. I was happy to have shelter for the time being. I knew it was not permanent; I had no identification papers, and they did not have enough food to fed me.

I proved to be a fast worker, and I knew a little bit about farming because of my experience at the forester's house. Every day, I went out with the farmer and his wife to gather potatoes from their few acres of land. We dug them up and brought them to the cellar to store for the winter. I also helped with chores around the house.

The Jablonskis also appreciated my extra help with their seven-year-old daughter. She was approaching the time of her first Holy Communion, and I offered to tutor her. Of course, I knew nothing about the catechism she was studying but saw this as a great opportunity to learn about the Catholic way of life.

"Get your catechism," I would tell her whenever I had some free time, "and meet me in the barn."

First I instructed the girl to cross herself. "Again," I would say, didactic like a teacher. I had her repeat the motions over and over until I too had rehearsed them well in my head. I also learned all the prayers. I would have to know them perfectly in order to live among Catholics as one of them, undetected. By the time the little girl knew her catechism by heart, so did I.

In the meantime, I was also improving my Polish. I lost all remaining traces of my Yiddish accent as well as other indications of my Jewish past. I lost my Jewish mannerisms, spoke softly without the use of my arms or hands, and maintained a humble demeanor. I tried to forget that I was even born a Jew, hiding my Jewishness beneath a hard crust. And I wondered every moment I was alive why it must be this way.

The Jew, the wanderer is he,
The homeless wandering Jew.
It's been ever thus.

I didn't feel safe on the Jablonskis' farm. I didn't feel far enough away from the ghetto of Brześć. My thoughts were always with those I had left behind. During the nights, a few Jews who had found a way to escape the ghetto roamed the countryside, starving. They scrounged subsistence as best they could, hiding during the day, coming out to forage for food toward evening. They would tap on the windows, begging for food. How I pitied them and wanted to help, but I dared not, lest I arouse suspicion. My heart ached for them, but there was nothing I could do. I will always carry some measure of guilt to my grave for putting my own safety ahead of all other considerations.

Before the year 1940 came to an end, a new law was enacted which required everyone, even little children, to carry identification. When Mr. Jablonski told me about the law, I said that I would go to my hometown to get my papers and would return to work as soon as possible. The next day, he took me to the train station in the nearest town, and we parted for what I knew would be the last time.

I did not know what to do with myself. I had no place to go and no way to feed myself. Without papers, I would be suspect.

I chose to return to Biała Podlaska, hoping that I would meet someone I knew—perhaps someone remained there who could help me. But when I arrived, I was so afraid to move around the town that I stayed on the train and rode back to Brześć. Then I returned to Biała Podlaska. Back and forth. Back and forth. I filled my time with train rides, sleeping in the train stations, stealing scraps of food or buying just enough to sustain me, thanks to some money hidden in the lining of my coat by my brother Abraham ages ago. He had told me then, "You may need this money in a dark hour. Do not be too generous with it. Use it only when there is no other way." Eventually, I knew this would arouse suspicion among the authorities. The Soviets had come into Eastern Poland as well as the Germans, and I learned our region was considered to be inside the Belorussian territory. Ukrainian police, who were collaborating with the Nazis, were considered especially violent. I wanted to avoid them as much, if not more, than the Germans.

● ● ●

I needed a destination, so I decided to return to the forester and his wife, my first Christian friends. When I got there, they gave me the same look I had seen on Fela's face: they had thought me dead. The warm air and the smells of freshly cooked food reminded me of my hunger and of the warmth and comfort and security I had missed for so long. Out of pity, they fed me and put me to bed immediately, near the oven, where I slept the sleep of the truly weary.

When I awoke in the morning, we talked about the liquidation of the ghettos of Biała Podlaska and Brześć.

They felt very sorry for me, expressed their wish to keep me there, but alas they could not. They had already told the neighbors that I was Jewish to explain why I had left. They said that I would have to leave soon, because hiding a Jew was punishable by death. They did not want to lose their lives, and I could not in good conscience put them at risk. I asked them if they knew any way for me to escape death or capture. They shrugged their shoulders, their eyes filled with pity. They clearly thought my time would come soon, that I would end up captured.

I also had been replaced. There was another girl living with them. Her name, they said, was Sabina Mazurek.

I had the impression that if it was not known that I had Jewish blood in my veins, they would have made room for me; my appearance was Polish enough for them. But they didn't want to risk getting caught.

Sabina was working in the field when I arrived. I rifled through her belongings and found her birth certificate. She was five years older than me, born on a farm in the country, and she was Catholic. A birth certificate was the identification I needed to pass through the next doors of destiny. I stuffed it into my pocket, grabbed one of Sabina's hats, and left the Wisniewskis' house after a sorrowful farewell. At least this time I had obtained a key to my survival.

Once again I was on my way to nowhere, exposed for any witness to turn me over to the Germans. I walked hurriedly through the meadows and forests back to Biała Podlaska, through the empty streets, to where the dim train station beckoned me.

Sabina Mazurek, born 1920, in Sitnik near Lublin, I practiced silently as again I rode the train aimlessly between

Biała Podlaska and Brześć. I had yet another name, this time with a proper document. This would be my new identity.

I decided to try my luck in Brześć. I left the train station and went to town, looking for ads for work. I noticed a sign in the window of a grocery store. The Polish family that owned the store was seeking a babysitter for their three-year-old daughter. Desperate for anything, I applied for the job. A beautiful, Aryan-looking young couple interviewed me. They were about thirty years old, and both were tall, with blond hair and blue eyes.

My Polish appearance and unaccented speech were not enough to convince them that I was truly Sabina Mazurek. They knew that many Jews were escaping from ghettos, and they wanted to be certain they weren't harboring one. My heart pounded as they examined my new birth certificate: Could they tell it wasn't really mine? Did I look aged enough to pass for five years older than I truly was?

"We want you to take care of our little girl," the man said. "Just don't let me find out that you are a Jew."

I feigned a horrified look. "Oh no!" I protested. "I am a Christian, a Catholic, born and raised among pious churchgoers." I crossed myself to prove my point. It seemed to help.

When they brought me home, I thought I was in heaven. The apartment was well furnished and clean. From the kitchen came delectable smells that awakened my ever-empty stomach. A maid was in charge of the many pots and pans, which she filled with wondrous treats: rolls and cakes, meat and potatoes. I marveled at my surroundings; I had landed in luxury.

And then a thought came. How many of the beautiful objects I saw before me had been taken from Jews? Was the mahogany furniture the prized possession of some Jewish bride? Who had first slept on those thick down pillows and been kept warm by the down blankets? Who had surprised their Jewish wife by bringing home such a richly colored sofa?

I shoved these questions aside. For the moment, I was fortunate to be there. I had a bed to sleep on—a wood-framed, folding army cot—and plenty to eat. Such luxuries, after being homeless and starving for weeks. And all I had to do was care for one adorable little girl with curly, blond hair and long lashes framing her baby-blue eyes.

My only source of discomfort was my new employers' persistence in their search for my true identity. Could they sense my fear, like bloodhounds stalking their prey? They continually tried to find someone to verify the fact that I was really Sabina Mazurek.

It was decided that they would go to church on Sunday morning, and I would take the little girl in the afternoon. In my heart, I was none to happy about this arrangement, because this would be my first time in church, and I was not sure I would know how to conduct myself properly. Still, I made them think I was thrilled to attend.

They returned from church and happily announced that they had found a girlfriend of mine there. "She was so glad to hear you are among us," the man told me. "She said she has not seen you in a very long time."

She has never seen me, I thought, desperate to conceal

my terror. I was sure that I would be led to the Gestapo within the hour and that would be the end of me. I wore a mask of joy. "I can't wait!" I told them, trying to act as if I looked forward to seeing an old friend.

"Well, you won't have to wait long," the woman said with a gleam in her eye. I couldn't tell whether she was genuinely excited by the thought of my happy reunion or whether she was thrilled by the prospect of exposing me if I turned out to be a fraud. During the short weeks I had been there, I had never felt she trusted me.

"Your friend will come here this afternoon," she said. "She will show you the way to church. You can attend the later mass together."

"That's lovely," I exclaimed, glad to have at least a short reprieve, one which would give me a chance to fill my basket with food and leave while my employers were off working at their store.

Unfortunately, Sabina's friend was eager and came early. Of course she did not recognize me, and she began asking me questions about their hometown. I could not answer a single one. She left, presumably to head for the grocery store that belonged to my employers, so I expected they would be back to confront me in minutes. I grabbed some food, abandoned the little girl in the apartment, and dashed down the single flight of stairs and out the door, putting as much distance between myself and my short-lived paradise as possible.

• • •

Again, I did not know where to go and what to do. I was

SABINA

afraid to remain in Brześć, so I returned again to Biała
Podlaska. I had an urge to revisit the last place I had been
with my family. I went all the way to the building in the
empty ghetto where we had shared our cramped living
quarters. I did not dare go to our old apartment but,
instead, continued up to the top floor and across the hall
to where the ghetto boundary ended. It was where the old
volksdeutsch couple lived. When I first came to the ghetto
with my family, she was one of the neighbors that I'd visit
regularly. I knocked.

"Bella!" she cried when she opened the door. She
covered her mouth in amazement and pulled me quickly
into her apartment, recognizing her own folly. "Quickly,
come inside."

I resisted her pull just enough for her to perceive my
apprehension.

"Don't worry. He's not here." She was referring to her
husband.

It was a relief to be in the company of a woman who
knew I was Jewish and did not care. She and her husband,
as German nationals, had received special treatment from
the Nazis. They had plenty of food and were the first to be
hired for privileged positions. There were many times I had
visited her, dispirited and hungry. The woman would feed
me and provide me with a little solace from the pressures of
the ghetto. Seeing her was comfort all over again.

Her drunken husband was a baker who worked nights
and slept all day. The woman assured me she would be able
to hide me from him should he wake up while I was there.
She took one look at me and saw how dirty, hungry, and
frightened I was. She immediately prepared something to

eat for me and offered me a chance to wash up and rest for a bit. Then she told me something that had me shaking with excitement.

"There is a very small number of Jewish workers, men, who are led in and out of the ghetto to work every day."

Could the group include anyone I knew? Perhaps Abraham or Joseph?

The following morning at 6:30, I stood on a street corner just outside the ghetto of Biała Podlaska, waiting, watching for this group of workers. Although I knew that my hopes were probably unfounded, I had to see if one of my brothers might be among them.

My hand was in my pants pocket, clutching the precious birth certificate.

But for the sounds of heavy shuffling and dragging in the distance, the entire area was eerily quiet. No other living souls were on the streets of the ghetto. They must have evacuated everyone.

As I stood in silence, deep in my thoughts, I could almost hear the lamentations of those who had once lived there—ghosts, victims' voices were screaming, begging for revenge. I felt like shouting back to them in Heaven, that they were not forgotten by those still living. A lump formed in my throat as I struggled with the agony of memory.

The work group passed near me, chained and heavily guarded. I strained to see if I could recognize anyone. How pathetic they looked, like skeletons, tattered, many barely able to keep up, forcing themselves on, knowing if they did falter, they would be killed on the spot. My brothers were not among them. I continued to stand there, immobilized, lamenting the fact that the time had come for me to let go of my family, my past, and my despair.

Before I had a chance to leave my perch, the Nazi guards sensed me and shot at me. I ran like the blazes, easily outpacing any man burdened by official military gear. If they had had a dog, they would have caught me.

I escaped back to the *volksdeutsch* woman's apartment, but she told me I couldn't stay long. "My husband must not find you here."

A brief but filling bite to eat, and I went—to wander again.

The shadow of death followed me everywhere, but in public, I had to appear happy at all times, pretending not to have a care in the world. I was entering a new and different world, a world of make-believe. My acting assignment was a fateful one.

Perform the role well, Sabina, and your reward at the end of each scene will be life.

Death would be my fate should I slip out of character at any time. I was the sole performer as well as the director of the show, for there was no one I could trust to guide me.

The winter of 1940/1941 was a hard time. During the days I roamed the streets of German-occupied Biała Podlaska like a lost, dirty dog, rejected by her owners and vulnerable to the dogcatchers.

At night, I loitered at the train station, where I forced myself to stay awake for fear of exposing my identity by talking in my sleep. I was dizzy with emotion, exhausted from the constant, unsettled moving. I hoped that I could blend in with the many people waiting for trains, which never ran on schedule. Sometimes people had to wait many days for trains to arrive. I pretended to be among them, awaiting a train that would carry me into the unknown.

I prayed for consolation and relief and thought nothing of the future, only of each day as it came upon me. With me I carried my riches: the small, round basket that I had brought with me from the ghetto and that contained about half a loaf of dark bread and some scraps of fabric.

The hours passed quickly. As curfew came, I envied

those who walked into their warm houses, and doubled my efforts to keep my coat buttoned securely. I heard them locking the doors behind them. Life for them went on as usual. With night coming on, I wished I had never been born a Jew.

A tornado of thoughts whirled around my mind. For short periods, I managed to forget the great danger that surrounded me by allowing myself to dwell in fantasies. In my mind, I went back to the warm, comfortable home where I had been treated with loving care and had been given everything a girl could want. My thoughts took me back to my youth—how I longed to remain there forever.

A blanket of sorrow slowly wrapped itself around my entire being and pulled me back to the place where I stood, in the no-man's land between death and despair, on an almost-empty street. *Please God*, I prayed as always, *please lead me to safety*.

One night, a group of smugglers was moving quickly along the street. I decided to attach myself to this roving band, to go wherever they were going. With my torn clothing and small, round basket, I probably looked like a smuggler myself. I was only missing wares to sell.

The group reached the train station, and I was glad that the guards did not notice me as we passed. Had they suspected me of smuggling or being homeless, they would have subjected me to questioning, which, in my dispirited state, I was not sure I could have survived. I welcomed the cool, hard surface of the wooden bench that was my bed for the night.

While roaming the streets of Biała Podlaska, I happened to get closer to the heavily guarded group of Jewish workers. They looked more like shadows than humans, barely able to move, using their last strength to just stay alive. My hand twitched as I yearned to give them the last morsel of bread that was in my basket. There is always a look about those who have given up. It's in the eyes. These workers looked pitifully at every passerby, saying silently that they were ready to give up, that their lives and hopes hung by a thread

Dear God, I thought, *who knows better than I the fate of my fellow Jews? Who understands their desperation better than I?*

I longed for the ability to help preserve a single shred of the beautiful Jewish life I had once known. I wished, with tears in my eyes and a weight on my heart, that I could open my mouth and persuade the peasants I was walking with to please save those people, but no sound came out. To speak would have been to betray my own identity.

The scene was so pitiful that even a stone could have been moved to pity. A peasant woman threw a loaf of bread into the group. Immediately, I did the same. Once she had opened the door, I could allow myself to walk through it. I found more bread and threw it to them too.

Soon they were taken away, and I continued to stand there, alone with my sorrow. At that moment, I decided to remain in Biała Podlaska, although it could mean risking my life, in order to supply this poor group with bread and water. It became a goal, a reason to live.

I came back every day. But one day I came to the place where they worked, and they were no longer there. Their job was over.

There was no longer any reason to remain in Biała Podlaska. I was sure that the big town was now clear of Jews.

I prayed to God: *Where should I go now? Is there any secret passage to lead me to safety?* I had the birth certificate of Sabina Mazurek, and I was trying to forget my Jewish origins. I would probably have converted to Christianity if there had been someone to help me with the preparations, and if it would have helped guarantee my survival. I still remembered the Catholic prayers by heart, and I would have promised to be a good Christian, had I been able to trust someone with my secret.

A new day started, with new troubles. I had no plans and no place to go. I wandered around like a vagabond, joining a group of peasants here, ducking into doorways there. I hated the day yet wished the night would never come. Back home, I had been afraid of the dark. By now, I was comfortable with the dark; death could come as easily in the light.

Early on this day, I was stopped by a guard. Someone must have pointed me out to him. He barked angrily, "What is your name? Show me your identification!"

I told him my name was Sabina Mazurek and handed him my birth certificate. He tested me by asking where Sitnik was. Apparently he was satisfied by my answer, because he just said, "Why don't you just stay home?"

I told him I would, and he let me go. I was relieved, but I still looked back over my shoulder as I walked away. I was more frightened than ever before, having lost my last refuge: my anonymity. I searched for some trace of hope, some idea of how to deal with my situation, but no solution came to mind.

I thought of visiting the forester and his wife, frantic with hope that they might help. I was desperate for a piece of my previous life, when there had been some freedom from worry. I walked from one village to another, with only the winds of snowstorms coming out to meet me.

I was also forever plagued by the fear that the real Sabina had reported the theft of her birth certificate and the police would find me and put me to death for robbery. Many times I wondered if she was the real Sabina or if she too was a Jewish girl who had assumed another identity. I hoped that she was the real Christian girl by that name. It would be easier for her to get another authentic birth certificate.

My guilty conscience also would not let me rest. I decided to return to the forester's house to make sure it was all right with them that I continued to use Sabina as my alias. Would they hold my crime against me?

When I came to the house, Mrs. Wisniewska was preparing supper. Again, she was astonished to see me alive. She quickly whisked me out of the house, offering no respite or food, and warning me that Sabina knew I had taken her birth certificate. She advised me to leave Biała Podlaska immediately.

I did as she instructed. In a semiconscious state, exhausted, and sore, I walked on. I was so terribly homesick and wished so much for a little encouragement and guidance. However it came, be it from a shadow or ghost, I would have welcomed the chance to take the heavy load of responsibility off my shoulders, even just for a while. I felt so bitter, so dumb, and so inexperienced. Had any living soul stopped to ask me anything, I am sure I would have poured out my sorrow, for I could no longer contain it.

Yet to draw any attention to myself, to speak to anyone, could easily have brought disaster. I thought, *you have been given this test, and you must go on by yourself. Death surrounds you; it is constantly challenging you, constantly closing in.*

Fortunately, no one approached me along the way to the train station. Alone, I held myself together.

Following Mrs. Wisniewska's advice to leave town, I snuck past the guards one last time and boarded a train to Warsaw, the only place I could think of going. I had been there as a child, with my father, on days when I was on vacation from school. He had introduced me to the wholesalers with whom he dealt. In my desperation, I imagined that maybe I could find some of those people and they would be kind to me, for the sake of my father. I remembered how well they had treated me as a child and how much they had liked my father.

The train pulled out of the station and began a journey that lasted two or three days. I wished the train would never stop; I had no plans for my tomorrow.

I pretended to sleep and changed seats frequently to avoid conversation with the strangers around me. I must have looked like a typical smuggler, holding a peasant's basket that might have been filled with eggs, butter, cream, cheese, and other goods that could be sold at a premium in Warsaw.

I must have really fallen asleep, or perhaps I was deep in thought, when I heard a husky voice, "Miss. Miss. What is your name?"

I turned toward the voice, still in a daze. Before me stood a middle-aged woman, slightly hunched over. Her face was red, like that of a drunk. She was interested in my basket. Perhaps I looked naïve enough to sell her my wares below the market price.

"Are you on your way to Warsaw?" she asked.

"Yes." I spoke quietly and prayed she would leave me alone.

"Do you have a steady dealer for your products?"

"Yes," I said, shifting in my seat.

"What do you usually sell?" She was persistent.

"Eggs, butter, cream, and vodka," I fibbed, surprised by my own quick thinking.

The woman wanted to see the contents of my basket. "Just let me take a look at them. If the eggs are large and the butter is fresh, I will pay you a higher price than your regular dealer."

I told her that I had already promised another young woman, who was a good friend. I insisted that I could not disappoint her. Besides she would be waiting for me at the station in Warsaw.

I clung to my little basket, praying for a way to keep it away from the woman smuggler.

At dusk, the train screeched stubbornly to a halt.

"Warsaw," announced the conductor.

Numb with fear, I stood motionless until the crowd propelled me off the train. I had no idea where to go.

Suddenly, I heard the gruff voice of the woman smuggler again. "Is she here?"

For a moment, I didn't remember whom she was talking about. "No, but I'm sure my friend will be here soon."

"You don't have time for that," the woman told me. "The curfew will be in effect in a few minutes and all the buildings will be locked for the night. Do you know where she lives?"

"Of course."

"Then you will go to her in the morning. Tonight you stay with me."

I knew this was yet another ploy to get to my goods, but I had no choice. For the moment, at least, I would be off the street and would not be arrested.

The woman treated me to tea and some unrecognizable food in the evening, and then treated herself to quite a bit of vodka. She fell asleep in a drunken stupor, and I covered myself with a down comforter and slept well for the first time in weeks. I suspect that she figured out sometime in the night that I carried nothing of value in my basket, yet she did nothing to me. She didn't turn me in to anyone, never said anything about it. In the morning, I quickly thanked her and let myself out while she sat on a stool, her back to me as she peeled potatoes, preparing her breakfast.

On my first day in Warsaw, I found myself homeless again. In the early morning light, the road was strangely lifeless. The few figures I saw through the wintry, misty snow seemed more like mannequins than real people. Soon I came to a main street, where people walked to and fro on their way to work. Some stood in clusters, waiting for buses. Others spilled out of streetcars.

I walked, pretending I had a destination, absently admiring the pretty displays in the storefronts. I passed a butcher shop, a bakery, and a corner grocery like the one my mother's cousin once owned. It was between our house and the river in Serock, and whenever I went by, she would offer me one of the delicious blueberry sweet rolls she baked.

The streets of Warsaw were strewn with beggars and peddlers. I envied them despite their poverty, because unlike me, at least they had a place to sleep at night. I kept walking, hoping for a miracle, thinking, *Oh please, let me find a place to stay, some little corner to shelter me.*

With evening fast approaching, I found myself at the beginning of Jaworowska, a street lined with buildings of various sizes. At one corner stood a woman selling a scanty selection of wilting soup greens: two carrots, a stalk of celery broken into smaller pieces, and some parsley. She looked old but, as I learned later, was really only in her forties. Poverty and hardship had aged her prematurely, and she was almost totally blind. I became her best customer that day, using the few coins in my pocket to purchase her vegetables, one item at a time. To me, this was a gourmet meal.

I bought until she ran out of stock. In the meantime, we became acquainted. She told me about her twelve-year-old daughter and her sixteen-year-old son, for whom she would buy bread and milk with the money she made selling vegetables.

As she turned to leave for home, I caught my breath and blurted out the question that had been burning in my throat. "Do you know anyone who is looking for a boarder?"

I explained to her that I had come from a farm and was looking for work in the city and, in the meantime, needed a place to sleep. I said I had always dreamed of coming to Warsaw, and now that I had arrived, I did not want to have to go back home. I told her I would pay for my room and board just as soon as I had found a job.

The woman said that she would rent me a spot in her one-room house. She had an extra army cot I could sleep on. Overjoyed to get off the street, I followed her home. Every moment of safety gave me enough time to rebuild my courage and hope—until the next stroke of fortune.

We walked up and down steep hills for miles, dodging holes in the broken ground. I had always envisioned Warsaw as a wealthy and beautiful city; now I was to discover how the poorer half lived. We walked through the filthiest, most desperate slum of town, and though I was hoping we would reach a nicer neighborhood, we stopped. The peddler's house was a shabby shack the size of a tool shed. In the middle of the room were two beds. A little cement stove stood in one corner, and a small table and bench were placed under the only window. The sparseness of the furnishings made the room seem large and bare.

Sitting on one bed was a skinny girl who looked younger than twelve. A vague smile passed over her shiny lips when she saw her mother. A bead of saliva dripped from her mouth as she opened it to eat her portion of the long, thin loaf of bread.

The boy rose slowly from his bed as we entered the room. He seemed much more alert than his sister but slothful, completely lacking energy or ambition. Apparently it was his job to care for his disabled sister while his mother worked all day to provide their meager meals.

The three of them gobbled their bread and gulped their milk standing up. I felt sorry for them, but still they were more privileged than I. When they finished their supper, it was already dark. By the light of the moon, the woman set up my cot and covered it with a flea-ridden blanket. I had no pillow and I used my coat as an additional cover to keep from freezing. After a day of constant walking and worrying, I fell fast asleep and did not awaken until morning.

Early the next day, I followed the woman over broken sidewalks, past garbage tossed randomly in the streets, back to the main part of town. From there, I wandered, from main street to side street, revolving around the peddler as the earth does the sun. I was afraid to stray too far from Jaworowska Street, lest she leave me behind. Her house had no address and I could not find it on my own.

"Please take me home again tonight," I begged. "I will find a job and then I will pay you for your generosity. Right now I simply have no money."

This was not quite true, for I still had some money in the hem of my coat. But what was left was American dollars. I thought this might be the time to use those dollars, but there was no one I could trust to exchange it for Polish zloty. If I went to a stranger with dollars, he might become suspicious. Once in a while, I would touch the spot where the money was hidden, imagining the food I could buy with it. I longed for my brother to be with me. He would know what to do. I felt so helpless.

In the evening, I returned to the blind woman's cold,

empty shack for a second time. In the morning, I again returned to the streets, venturing a little farther out in my orbit. I had to find work before the woman's patience ended.

On the fourth day, I noticed a sign in a large store window: "Advanced seamstress girl needed to help dressmaker." Immediately, I went to the address on the sign and applied for the job.

• • •

I had no real experience with a sewing machine or even a needle and thread. Mama had never tried to teach me. But in my desperation, I convinced myself that these skills were hereditary. With a mother who was a dressmaker and a father who repaired sewing machines, I thought I ought to be able to sew without any training.

As soon as I had introduced myself to the young dressmaker, she put me to the test. She handed me thread and a piece of fabric and instructed me to thread the sewing machine and sew a straight seam. I had played with my mother's machine enough to know how to do those two things fairly well.

"You will learn." The dressmaker was alluding to my less-than-perfect results.

At the outset, I was to work for bed and food as a helper. I accepted the job without a moment's hesitation. With no belongings to bring nor relatives to part from, I joined their household that very moment.

The dressmaker lived in a two-room apartment with her mother, her four-year-old son, and her younger, unmarried sister. I was given a bed in a little corner of the kitchen, separated from everything else by drapes. My work consisted of running errands and doing housework. I went to the store to buy thread, needles, pins, and material. My employer sewed bras and girdles. I did not do much sewing; I needed far more training than the dressmaker was willing to give me.

We all knew that the dressmaker's mother or sister could have done the errands and the housework; they really did not need me. I could see that in their kindness, they were trying to find a way to keep me on, perhaps until after the holidays. Until then, there would be much cleaning, cooking, and baking to do. We sang Christmas carols as we prepared the food and decorated the Christmas tree.

The sister often went on dates with her steady boy-friend. They celebrated New Year's Eve together, looking forward to a year of happy events. Perhaps, I surmised, they would be married before the end of 1942. I envied her beauty, her elegance, and her carefree life. Most of all, I envied her future. I knew that my arrangement would soon end. I could not do the more-skilled sewing that had been expected of me, so I was a burden.

The mother came home one day and told us about new arrests, mostly of the Polish intelligentsia, religious leaders, and aristocracy. She said the Germans were almost done with the Jews and the gypsies, and now they were taking away Polish priests and professors. Some of the prisoners had escaped and were returning to warn other Poles about the horrors of these camps.

The news was horrifying. *Is that where my parents went?* I wanted to scream with shock and grief, but instead, I pretended not to hear and not to care. Always, I had to act like the dumb peasant girl I claimed to be.

Oh, how I wished for the whole war to be over, for it all to end. I wished desperately for someone to pluck me out of this hell and plant me back in the past, where life was quiet, where dreams of the future were possible, where there was protection, where there was my caring family. I ached for the time when breathing was easy, when worries were few.

Soon after the holidays were over, in January 1942, I was dismissed. I packed my little basket and left.

• • •

The only place for me to go in Warsaw was back to the home of the blind peddler woman. I went back to the corner of Jaworoska Street, where she usually sold her carrots and celery. This time she was not there, perhaps because it was too cold. Snow had been falling all day. I circled the area for hours, hoping that it would stop snowing and the woman would return to her post.

As the last rays of sun shone on the thick, white blanket of snow, I set out to find the peddler's house. I walked alone against the strong, cold winds, the icy drizzle slapping my face. I felt the frost cut through my muscles as I was carried by the force of the storm. As if floating—for I could not feel my feet—I found my way to the bottom of the hill near the woman's house. I tried to find the right path, but none was visible. I stood at the edge of what seemed like an endless desert of snow.

The snow had filled the valleys, and the hills looked

like one high plane. One wrong step in any direction could have plunged me into the abyss of broken pavement. If I stood still too long, I was sure to turn into an icy mass.

Suddenly, the silhouette of a person appeared before me. He was an elderly man, bundled in heavy clothing. He asked me if I was lost.

"No sir," I said. "I am just trying to find the path that leads to those houses." I pointed toward the peddler's house.

The man motioned for me to follow him. "I know where it is." He spoke in a soothing voice. "Come with me. I'm going the same way."

The snow was up well beyond my ankles, seeping into my shoes, making my feet thoroughly wet, but I was so grateful to have a guide that I did not mind. Finally we reached the doorstep of the peddler woman's shack. As I thanked the strange gentleman for his help, I realized that I had another challenge ahead. How would I explain my disappearance? How could I expect her to take me back after I failed to pay her for my first stay?

I knocked on the door, shivering from the cold and the fear that I might be turned away. The son let me in, and mother and son asked me in unison where I had been.

"I met a friend and stayed with her a while."

"So you have not found work?" the peddler concluded, disappointed that I would not be able to pay her yet.

Silently, I put up my cot and went to sleep, unable to release my heavy burden by crying. I watched the peddler climb into bed with her daughter, and I thought again about my incredible loneliness.

Each day, I left the shack hoping to find a decent way to earn a living. Each night I returned to the shack pitiful, poor, workless, and helpless. The strange streets became my home during the day, and the empty shack became my resting place at night. Even this was a luxury I could not take for granted.

One night I was awakened by the warmth of a body pressing against mine. As I opened my eyes, I saw in the darkness that it was the boy. He was trying to push his way onto my cot, as if I should pay my way by offering myself to him. Disgusted, I somehow managed to release myself from his grasp. At daybreak, I took my basket and left the shack for the last time.

That afternoon, I approached a woman standing on Jaworowska #2 Street as the sun was getting ready to set. This woman, Mrs. Sawicka, was younger than the peddler and had a softer disposition.

"*Pani*," I said. "Do you know of anyone who would accept me as a boarder?"

"Yes," she said gently. "I do. As a matter of fact, I need someone to take care of my six-year-old son, Kazic, while I travel to and from the country to get us food to eat."

Mrs. Sawicka explained that her husband was a prisoner of war in Germany, and she hoped to join him there soon. Until then, I could stay with her.

"I will be glad to accept the position," I said. "I will do it in exchange for a place to sleep."

Mrs. Sawicka smiled and led me to her home.

My time with Mrs. Sawicka was comfortable and relatively uneventful. An agreeable woman, she traveled often, leaving her son, Kazic, with me when she went on short trips and taking him with her for the lengthy ones. I had a roof over my head, a warm bed, sufficient food, and sanitation facilities. When they were away, I spent my time wandering the streets or sitting in one of the neighbors' houses. I needed some kind of companionship. The neighbors, who thought I was a Polish girl who was separated from her family, felt sorry for me and tried to help me. Their company was pleasant, yet I kept my visits short. I was always afraid they might find some traces of Jewishness if we were together too long.

One day, signs appeared all over the city declaring that everyone—men, women, young, and old—must carry their *Kennkarte*, their official identification papers, at all times. Anyone caught without an official, stamped identification card would be presumed Jewish and put to death instantly.

The neighbors were abuzz with plans for complying with this new mandate. From them, I learned what I had to bring with me and where to go to obtain the official ID.

I had been putting off this frightening procedure, but I could do so no longer. On December 10, 1942, I decided to apply for an identification card. I headed for the magistrate. On the way, I passed a photographer's shop and had my pictures made.

The magistrate was quite a distance from Jaworowska #2. I walked and walked, well past the lunch hour, mentally preparing myself along the way. When I arrived, I found a long line of people that extended out the front door. I joined the line, my heart pounding in my chest. Alone, scared, cold, and now hungry, I waited and waited. I pretended to glance nonchalantly at the birth certificate in my hands as I diligently studied it. I might have to part with the valuable information source. Writing down my information was out of the question, as it would definitely raise suspicions. I had to commit it all to memory.

I've never even been to Sitnik. I wasn't even a twinkle in my parents' eyes on October 21, 1920. Who are the Mazureks, my alleged parents? What do they look like? What kind of parents were they? Are they still alive? Do they worry about their daughter? What is this religion I profess to be a part of?

The line moved forward. I was inside the building.

I felt panicky; I wanted to scream, to release my pent-up tension, to shout out the truth and tell everyone who I really was. "I cannot pretend anymore! Please stop hunting me! I miss my family! I need to go home!"

Afraid of my own thoughts, at least I tried to control my trembling hands. *Will someone notice my fear? Will an informer recognize me as a Jew? Dear God! At any moment, someone may walk up to me and say, "You are a Jew. Come with me to Gestapo headquarters."*

How I wished I could disappear. *This is just a bad dream,* I tried to convince myself. *Soon someone will open a door for me and lead me to a place of safety. Perhaps there is a tunnel that will lead me away. I would be glad to crawl into even the darkest, dead-end, underground passage just to have a chance to sort out my crazy, mixed-up thoughts.*

I felt like escaping, like running back down through the throngs of people behind me in line, out of the building. But there was no running now.

I have come a long, long way, and I must not give up now. I must not make one foolish mistake. Afraid of death, afraid of darkness, afraid of my own shadow and my own thoughts, I leaned back against the cold, damp wall, waiting for my turn to face the officials.

My thoughts whirled as I climbed up the three flights of stairs, one or two steps at a time, toward the desk on the top floor. Each step felt like the rung of an unsteady ladder, about to crash to the earth.

I would be questioned by German and Polish officials; they would be able to read my mind. They would deliver a verdict. They would seal my fate, either by confiscating my birth certificate and revoking my right to live, or by allowing me to put my signature on the bona fide identification card of Sabina Mazurek.

The people above me seemed like vultures, ready to

devour me. Below me it was a pit of snakes ready to strike. Everyone I saw looked like a beast eager to tear me to pieces.

I wondered if there were other hidden Jews in the line. I hoped so. I hoped that others had managed to survive. As doomed as I felt, I realized that I was luckier than most. I had several sources of camouflage: my small, slightly turned-up Koszciuszko nose and my flawless Polish accent. I had been deliberately lifting all my Jewishness out of my being, hiding it somewhere far away, out of even my own reach.

I wished there was someone else I knew in line with me. I looked again at the continual stream of people. I wished I could trust someone and share my fears, if only by a subtle exchange of glances. But short tempers and friction were the rule in the dark hallway and the endless, steep staircase. Children were crying and adults were arguing. No unity there, just a modern-day Tower of Babel, where the brotherhood of man was lost in fear and selfishness.

I felt a strange sensation, as if my soul were being lifted out of my body, floating into oblivion. *I must forget about Bella,* I reminded myself. *I must let go of her, leave her and slam the door on her. I am Sabina now.*

I became hypnotized by this mantra: *I am Sabina.* I stared blankly as I reached the front of the line, stiff as a convict awaiting sentencing. I turned in my birth certificate and, as if possessed, answered questions and signed my name without thinking.

"Wait here," the clerk in the green Nazi uniform ordered.

Oh dear God, I prayed silently. *Please get me out of this trap.*

I was ready to bolt. I was almost positive that the clerk would return with a Gestapo agent and they would take me away or shoot me on the spot. Instead, the clerk returned with a *Kennkarte* all ready for me to sign. Holding the pen as steadily as I could, I signed the long-awaited document "Sabina Mazurek." Sweat poured down my back in pure relief and the color came back to my cheeks.

The clerk inked my fingers and pressed them onto the document, much as they did with the official stamp a moment later. I was giddy. Now I could go home and show the gray, trifold cardboard document to Mrs. Sawicka, to the neighbors, to anyone. It was one more layer of protection. I now had proof of being both Catholic and Polish—or at least proof that government clerks believed that I was.

The next time I opened my eyes, I was back in the street, my new identification card in hand. I had no recollection of descending the long staircase.

• • •

Living with Mrs. Sawicka and possessing a proper ID left me feeling more solid than I had in a long while, but I did not believe it could hold. I was still living in Poland, surrounded by Poles, and there was always a chance that someone would recognize that I was not the Sabina they knew from Sitnik. I knew nothing about that town, could not reproduce its accent—if it had one—or describe its personality or environs. Wherever I was, I was most in danger from other Poles. I had to consider my options.

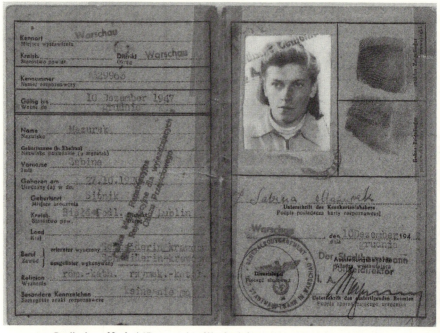

Bella's official ID card with Sabina Mazurek's name
and Bella's photo. This ID card allowed her to assume
Sabina's identity during the war.

One day, I passed a sign that read:

REGISTER TO WORK IN GERMANY.
UNDER GOOD CONDITIONS
YOU WILL GET SPECIAL PRIVILEGES
IF YOU REGISTER WILLINGLY

Germany: the eye of the storm. I went into the office to inquire, and before I realized what was happening, I had been accepted as a volunteer. The officials took my name and address, and they told me that I would receive notice of my departure date.

Once I had time to think about it, I was not at all sure I had done the right thing. *Go to Germany? To the Nazis' lair? How ironic that this Jewish girl should choose Germany as a destination.*

When I arrived home, I told Mrs. Sawicka what I had done. She believed I had done the right thing, because it was very hard to find work in Warsaw. She was planning to do the same thing.

Summoning great courage and trusting in my *Kennkarte* ID, I awaited notice from the immigration office. Finally, I was summoned to appear on April 20, 1943.

In May 1943, the day before I was to leave Warsaw, something amazing happened. For the first time in two years, I spoke with someone who knew my true identity—not just that I was Jewish, but knew me to my core, had known me as a child in Serock. Bella Laska, my old friend and neighbor. Our encounter was way too brief.

I had thought I had seen her once before from a

Bella's official volunteer work permit issued by
the German Reich, allowing Sabina Mazurek to
work in Germany, dated May 1943.

distance and had been sure I was hallucinating, but the fleeting figure had slipped away before I could check. This time I noticed her as I returned home from my last walk on Marshal Kowska Street. She was among a group of people waiting on a corner for a streetcar, standing in the deepening shadow of a tall building.

I rushed over and stopped right in front of her, my feet planted as if cemented to the ground. Instantly entranced, I could not move a muscle. All of the blood rushed to my brain, which was working at full capacity to ascertain her identity quickly, lest I make a fatal error. Could she be who I thought she was?

There was no doubt. It was Bella Laska. Only a brick wall had separated our homes. I had watched her for hours, memorizing the way she combed her long hair that gleamed in the sunlight. She had looked like a princess from a storybook, a goddess in my eyes. She had been so graceful then, sitting on the steps that led down to her parents' grocery store.

I recognized her round, blue eyes, clear as the sky on a summer day. I recognized her long, dark lashes and the deep dimples in her cheeks. I recognized the hands that had helped my beloved mother in the kitchen on Friday afternoons.

Bella Laska stared back blankly for an agonizing minute and then sprang forward and grabbed me under the arm. The bystanders looked at us in astonishment. We easily could have aroused suspicion. At any moment, an informer could report our strange behavior to the authorities. In complete silence, she ushered me to the nearest cafeteria.

We sat down at a corner table and she ordered some

rolls and two cups of coffee. "What is your name *now?*" she asked.

"Sabina," I told her, following her cue. "Sabina Mazurek. And what is yours?"

"Kristina Karmen."

My whole body was trembling. Nothing seemed real. I could not believe she was at my side. My dear childhood friend Bella Laska reached over the table to hold my hand. Her touch calmed the core of my being. We sat holding hands, staring at each other like lovers.

"You have changed so much in the last four years," she whispered. "I did not recognize you at first. You were just a child before the war, and look at you now. You are a young lady already."

Ignoring the danger, we plunged into a rapid discussion.

"Sabina, I got married a few months ago, but I have already lost my husband. Thoughts of revenge are all that keep me going. I am working for the resistance, falsifying identification papers and helping Jews escape from the ghetto. Do you have an ID?"

"Yes." I spoke in the same hushed tone. "But I am afraid it is not good. I stole a birth certificate for a Polish Catholic girl and used it to get a *Kennkarte*. I can't stop worrying that the real Sabina is still alive and that she will find out and stop my papers. Can you help me?"

"Sabinka! Sabinka!" Bella said, her musical voice rising whimsically. "I wish I could get papers like yours. Yours is the real thing—it is original, authentic. Our papers are not. We have people who work at the magistrate, who steal blank forms. Jewish experts forge the director's signature. If any of these documents were to fall into the wrong hands and were examined carefully, they would be caught. There would be no way to verify the date of birth and other information we fill in; it is totally made up. You don't know how lucky you are. I am very proud of you."

Like a student who has been praised by her favorite teacher, I felt my chest swell and could not help smiling. I trusted her; she was so bright, so worldly. She had already graduated from high school when the war began. I thought about what she had just said, and then a jarring realization popped into my head. "What did you say about sneaking Jews out of the ghetto? What ghetto?"

"The ghetto here in Warsaw."

I was dumbfounded. I had been living in Warsaw for over a year. I had roamed the streets for miles. I thought I knew the city, but I had no idea there was a ghetto. When I was lonely and homeless, I probably would have gone to join my brethren had I only known they were there.

Bella took out a pen and a scrap of paper and jotted something down. "I must go." She spoke in a louder voice, handing me the note. "I am late for an appointment. Here is my phone number. Call me if I can do anything for you."

My heart sank. "I am leaving tomorrow." I explained that I had volunteered to work in Germany and that my orders had arrived—I was to report the following day.

"Then we will spend tonight together," she said. "Call me in an hour and we will make plans."

I rushed home to Jaworowska #2 and told Mrs. Sawicka that I had met a friend. "Since I am leaving for Germany tomorrow, may I invite my friend to stay with me tonight?"

Mrs. Sawicka agreed. She had been very supportive

of my decision to volunteer, and she saw no harm in me having a happy farewell.

I called Bella Laska and she came to Jaworowska #2. She walked confidently into the room, past the tiny wooden bench with the washbasin and the cup.

"How do you do?" Bella addressed Mrs. Sawicka cordially. "I'm Kristina."

Mrs. Sawicka nodded and motioned toward the two chairs beside the table.

"I've brought some sweet rolls!" Kristina announced as we sat down.

Kazic sat on the bed, relishing the treat that Kristina handed him. Mrs. Sawicka set the teakettle on the iron stove, whose huge, black pipes provided the only contrast to the gray walls and the cement floor.

When all the tea had been drunk, Mrs. Sawicka undressed and put pajamas on her son, and the two of them retired to the bed they shared. Bella and I stayed awake all night, lying on the narrow sofa together, whispering. With Mrs. Sawicka sleeping a few feet away, we did not have much privacy, but the rewards, the sheer joy of talking together, outweighed any risk.

I needed to find out if I had been right about seeing her before.

"Yes," she said. "That probably was me. I often pass this block, and I remember once having the feeling that someone was watching me. I ducked into the tall building just down the street."

"Then it was you! Oh how I wish I had caught up with you. We would have had more time together." Now that I had a friend, I longed to stay in Warsaw, to stay near her, to be taken care of for a change, to share our experiences and our sorrows. I needed the encouragement. She was the only beacon of light on my darkest road.

I also thought about the people she was helping. "I wish I hadn't volunteered to go to Germany. I could have helped you in the resistance."

Bella Laska shook her head. "No, this is for the best. I need to know you are safe. You must survive and tell everyone what happened to our townspeople, our community."

"How are the Jews doing in the ghetto? Are the Nazis planning to liquidate it soon, as they have so many others?"

She told me the Jews in the Warsaw ghetto understood their fate only too well, and they were planning a revolt. The starving, sickly inhabitants were going to rise up against their oppressors. Our people would not be annihilated without a fight. Some of the Nazis would have to die with them.

Bella was one of those with contacts outside the ghetto. With forged papers declaring her a Christian, she had access to a broader world and could move fairly easily about the city. Her job was to help others escape into the countryside, where they might have a chance at surviving, and to bring in as much support as she could to those remaining and to those planning the uprising. There were Jews and other partisan fighters, a whole network outside the ghetto with connections—money, false papers, food, and arms. Her role as an exchange agent was full of risks, but with her husband gone, she was as resolute as forged steel.

I could not believe my ears. I wanted to hear more details, but the sun was rising and our time together had to end.

—

Before Bella Laska left me at Mrs. Sawicka's apartment that morning, she went out and bought me a dozen sweet rolls and some other food to take on the train to Germany. She also left me some money.

"Remember my address," she instructed me. "Memorize it, then destroy the paper. Never write it down except on your letters to me."

With tears in our eyes, we kissed each other good-bye.

"I hope and pray," she whispered in my ear, "that God will continue leading you on a safe road. I know you can get through this. You are young and innocent, but you are strong."

There were not many preparations to be made, because all I owned was my little basket, which I filled with the food from Bella. With a heavy heart, I bid Mrs. Sawicka farewell.

At the volunteer station on Prosta Street, I waited with many others for them to deport us to our work positions. We were on a high floor in a long, dimly lit hallway; people of all ages sat on the floor or stood idly waiting. Someone next to me asked me my name and then told me hers. The building was filling up rapidly when two girls arrived. Suddenly, there was a commotion.

"What's happened?" I asked the person next to me.

"They took two Jews away," she said.

"They didn't look Jewish to me," I said, shrugging my shoulders to imply indifference.

"Well, someone pointed them out. And they did look a little too snobbish and elegant."

Two shots were fired in the courtyard, and we knew the girls were dead. *Dear God*.

Such discoveries were frequent and filled me with dread. I had heard about a girl who was living in Poland, working for a Catholic family. She was asked to prepare a chicken for dinner, and instead of dunking it in boiling water—which was not kosher, but was the non-Jewish way—she began to pluck its feathers. The woman of the house immediately recognized her as a Jew and reported her to the authorities.

Many Jews could pass outwardly as Gentiles, but their Yiddish accents gave them away. Sometimes they were betrayed by a habit, by using their hands too much when talking. In some cases, people can just tell. *The Poles can sense a Jew by smell and by appearance. And they show no mercy when they do.*

Hearing the gunshots, I was terrified. I looked over the gathered crowd and tried to calm myself, tried to remind myself that I fit well enough among the many Poles, old and young, sitting on the floor in there. I could not arouse suspicion at such a moment, when people were being studied. I tried to push my thoughts aside, to act carefree, but the laughing, animated Poles around me suddenly seemed unbearably sinister.

It was like the day I'd gone to get the *Kennkarte*. At any moment, I feared someone might say that they knew I was not from Sitnik, that they knew I was not really Catholic, that they knew Sabina and I was not really her.

Suddenly I heard shooting outside but from a different direction. Everyone rushed to the windows. I hadn't noticed but realized then that the windows overlooked what was clearly the Warsaw ghetto. We saw Jews fighting with German soldiers.

Looking out the window, I could see a big part of the ghetto below. I had a clear view of everything that was going on between the ruins and the tumbling walls. I could see German soldiers being carried out on stretchers. I thought of the work Bella Laska had done. I prayed for the Jewish inhabitants.

Jews were also being injured and killed. As they were gunned down, the Poles around me made comments, said that they deserved it.

I was torn between grief and fury. I wanted to scream. I wanted justice. I wanted to help the people of the ghetto. But I needed to stay silent, be the dumb peasant. That's all I was, all I could be—just a Catholic peasant. Had I cried or said anything, I would have been given away. What good would come of revealing myself? I could not help the Jews of the ghetto from where I was. I needed to stay on my path.

In spite of the fighting in the ghetto below, the procedure of transporting the workers to Germany continued uninterrupted. The Germans had each department running independently, so that a crisis in one would not interfere with the efficient work of another. Fighting in the ghetto and the transporting of the Polish workers to Germany had nothing to do with each other.

I paced back and forth, peering out the window as often as I felt I could without raising suspicion. I tried to look as bored with waiting as everyone else and hoped that my behavior would not betray my intense interest in the fighting below.

Soon, with a soul full of sorrow and pain, I followed the others as we were lead to the train station.

● ● ●

We finally arrived in Berlin. I had made small talk with my fellow travelers, so I said good-bye to a few, knowing I would never see them again, and then waited. The depot was crowded with trains, soldiers, and civilians. The steam from the trains and the rush of activity were overwhelming. There was an acidic, motor smell in the air. The speaker blared out announcements, orders—all in German. We stayed there for a long time, watching other groups of people get on and off trains. Several of us were told to remain on the same train until the next destination, Zeulenroda. When we arrived there, I was singled out and sent via a small motorbus to a nearby farming community called Langenwolshendorf, because my records showed that I had been born and raised on a farm and I had told my original recruiter that I would prefer to be on a farm—a farmer with a large farm in need of a good farm girl.

In Langenwolshendorf, I was picked up from the central office by Mr. Scheibe. He introduced himself to me, we shook hands, and off we went. I was on autopilot and said very little. I had no idea what was ahead of me, but tried to hide my nervousness. When I arrived at the Scheibes' farmhouse, I must have looked like a little animal cowering before a hunter.

But the minute I entered the house, my world changed. The welcoming smiles of both Mr. and Mrs. Scheibe assured me that they were satisfied with my appearance and apparent strength, and an atmosphere of peace and pleasantness abounded.

In one corner of the kitchen floor, there were newly hatched chickens, ducks, and geese. On the sofa near the table were two beautiful kittens playing happily. In this homey atmosphere, I forgot myself for a moment. I mentally lifted the veil of Sabina Mazurek and tasted but a drop of the Bella still inside.

I salute you, Bella. You have gotten this far.

• • •

The Scheibes had a comfortable home. The foyer to the house was very large and dark, capped by a high ceiling, with light shining down. To the right of the foyer was a door leading to the attic. Another door opened to the cellar, where the fruits and vegetables were stored for the winter. To the left were huge, brown, heavy doors leading to a large, white kitchen. There was a table in the middle of the room with at least twelve chairs. A huge chandelier hung from the ceiling. To the right in one corner was a white stove, and to the left a door opened to the laundry room. Inside the laundry room were washbasins and a large kettle to boil the clothes, and around the walls were built-in shelves for storage. There was a door to the pantry and more storage rooms. A steep staircase led up to the sleeping quarters and—what luxury—a bathroom with inside plumbing, hot and cold running water, and one large bathtub.

As I looked around, trying to seem pleasant and interested, like a hard worker, I notice Mr. and Mrs. Scheibe were watching with smiles. Again, I sensed some satisfaction, as if they were saying, "She has potential."

I had volunteered to work on a farm because I wanted to do physical labor outside. I felt safer outside. The vast sky above, the morning dew, the dawn, and the dusk, the open fields with their golden wheat, corn, and hay, the gardens filled with vegetables and fruit—all these gave me a respite from my unbearable fear of discovery and deep loneliness. They were my private paradise. I could be at one with nature, just as I was as a child, hiking in the meadows near my hometown. The Scheibe farm suited these needs, and as I settled in that first evening, I felt some hope that I had made the right decision coming here.

Because the Scheibes believed me to be a Polish Catholic peasant, I had to pretend that I did not understand their German. But the truth is that I comprehended their instructions better than the other foreign workers on the farm. The Scheibes thought that meant I was brighter. I was not. I just knew Yiddish, which is a mixture of German and Hebrew.

My pretense of not understanding their language served me well. My first evening on the farm, the Scheibes asked me to round up the geese that were running out the open gate into the dirt road. I was scared of geese after a terrible childhood experience, not so many years earlier in truth, when my curiosity had brought me too close to a gaggle in my neighbor's yard back in Serock. Our neighbor had a little farm where they raised a few cows, goats, sheep, chickens, geese, turkeys, and pigs. Often the smaller animals got out and went wandering into our yard. I was terrified of those creatures, especially the geese and turkeys. As if they sensed my fear, they had chased me, and I had run away as fast as I could, screaming in terror. They chased me out of my own yard.

Despite all the worse horrors I had faced, I was afraid to get in front of the Scheibes' geese for fear they too would chase me. I hesitated, then tried to round them up from behind. Comically, I only drove them farther away.

Fortunately, my new employers came to my aid, mistaking my ineptitude for misunderstanding the German language.

As far as Mr. and Mrs. Scheibe were concerned, I represented most Polish farmers. They were under the impression that I was from Poznan, which was annexed by the Reich. I told them that I had been separated from my family when we were evacuated, and I had gone to Warsaw. If another Pole had been present on my first morning at the farm, I would have been fingered as a fake. Fortunately, I was the only one there.

On the second day, the Scheibes started walking me through many of my chores. They took me to the cows and stood by my side to supervise as I sat down confidently on the low bench to begin milking the first cow. When they burst out in laughter, I was embarrassed and bewildered. What was I doing wrong? I quickly reviewed what Mr. Wisniewski, the forester in Biała Podlaska, had taught me: two fingers of each hand grasp the udder, squeeze, and pull.

Mrs. Scheibe sat down beside me and showed how to milk cows more efficiently, the "German way." Thinking that she had better retrain me from square one, Mrs. Scheibe taught me how to feed seed to the chickens and garbage to the pigs, how to gather eggs in the henhouse each morning, and how to work the ground to make it fertile. I learned to plow the fields and harvest the fruit. I helped with the berries, the apples, and the pears. The men did the heavy work, and Natalia, a foreign worker from Russia, and I did the sorting and cleaning.

The so-called "light" work was not without its hazards. Once, when trying to pull a tough sprout out of a potato, I tore the flesh under the nail of my right-hand ring finger. For days I ignored the sore, hoping it would heal itself. Finally, Mrs. Scheibe noticed that it was red and inflamed, and she insisted on going on her bicycle to bring the local doctor. The doctor wanted to open the infected flesh with a needle, in order to drain the wound. He knew I would object when I saw the needle, so he hid it from me for as long as possible. Mrs. Scheibe tried to distract me, but in the end, I spotted the needle as it came plunging toward my finger. Despite my many brushes with dangers far graver than a doctor's needle, I could not help panicking. I pushed the German doctor to the ground—to his and my astonishment. I still smile and cringe when I think what nerve I had!

Another time, I hurt my back while feeding the pigs. Mrs. Scheibe rode her bicycle to the drugstore to get me medicine, called in the doctor, and took over my chores for two weeks while I recovered. Natalia was beside herself. The lady of the house would never do such a thing for her. But the Scheibes had come to like me quite a lot. I never complained, never made demands, never acted moody in front of anyone. The façade worked. Mr. and Mrs. Scheibe perceived me as appreciative, quiet, and hardworking. To them, I was not at all like the other Polish and Russian workers in the area whose behavior reflected the pain of having been torn away from their families. Many had been caught on the streets, in the movie theaters, on the trains, and were sent to Germany as forced laborers without pay. I was a volunteer. I did my work cheerfully and productively. To the Scheibes, I seemed much like one of their local German girls.

Thus, unlike other foreigners, I was soon allowed to help with chores inside the house including cleaning and kitchen work. Every Tuesday I did the laundry—that was the worst. Although it was meant as a privilege, for me those were the hardest hours. At those times, Mrs. Scheibe could very well find me crying as I toiled over the wash-board. With a troubled expression, she would ask me if I preferred a different task. I always said no.

She probed, "What is upsetting you? Is our treatment unkind? Is the work too hard for your frail body? Are you hungry? Do you need more free time to socialize?"

I would shake my head and pretend not to understand. I could not let her figure out that I understood German. Also, the Polish workers in the area could not find out that I understood German. No one anywhere could even think I understood German or I would be doomed. But I appreciated her for asking. I wanted to tell her that my sadness was not her fault. She was not to be blamed, and I believed she was genuinely concerned about me. Were I able, I would have told her that I needed my freedom—the outdoors. I needed to work hard in the fields to forget my loneliness and homesickness. When I became isolated in a small laundry room, depression overtook me. And always, I thought of my family.

It was better when I was with the cows. Twice each day,

while milking the Scheibes' thirteen cows, I could block out the present with songs from the past. This was how I kept my true self alive, how I remembered who I really was. I would hum beautiful ballads of freedom, of suffering, of love, and of loneliness. Even on a dreary afternoon, the spring breezes seeping into the cracks of the barn, the clouds allowing the rays of the sun only a peek at the newly green fields, the rhythmic sounds of milk spraying the sides of the pail, of the cows chewing their cud and swishing their tails at the flies—all this made music flow from my war-weary heart.

Prychadila na birich Katiusha, prichadila na birich crutoy. I heard the words in my head as I hummed. They wrapped around me like my grandmother's warm embrace. *Climbing Kathy, on a steep, winding mountain, singing songs and greeting everyone from atop the mountain.* It was a Russian song that my grandmother taught me. I pictured my dear grandmother, Rivka, as she looked when she taught me that song: short and beautiful, despite the eye she kept closed ever since it had become blind. I loved to sleep at her house, to cuddle with her. Just being with her made me happy. She was all embracing, all accepting, all nurturing.

The only other time I could really let go was after the day's work was complete and I was alone in my room. Often the strain of the day and my homesickness overwhelmed me, and I buried my face in the fat feather pillows and huddled under the covers. Though I felt as if it all might tear me apart, my muffled cries did not penetrate the thick walls of my room to the rest of the house.

At night, huddled in the dark under my warm comforter, I thought of my mama. *If you were here with me today, I would tell you how much I love you. I did not tell you often enough. I don't remember saying, "thank you" for the sacrifices you made for me and for the rest of the family. If I could repay you, I would give my life to do so. I will survive this ordeal for you and because of you.*

One night I dreamed of my mama.

I am in the middle of a wide road. It is a clear day, chilly but sunny. The rays of the sun do not warm my flesh, nor can I catch a single breath of the fresh, crisp air surrounding me. I can see for miles, but there is nothing but road and sky. Where are the houses? Where are the fields? Are there no trees, forests, or birds here? Are there no people, no living things? There is nothing but empty space between the horizon and me. Fear and emptiness loom.

I am running. I can hear the clatter of their heavy boots. I look back impulsively, quickly. I can see them; I can see their long, green military coats and the rifles in their hands. They are aimed at me.

I can see the helmets on their heads, the painted swastikas mocking me.

They are closing in on me. I run faster and faster. Why am I not moving? Why do I seem to be running in place? In one minute, in a second, they will shoot. They will kill me. I will be dead in a minute. But why? Why do they want me dead? I do not want to die. I am only a teenager.

I am running faster and faster yet. I have to find a new place to hide. I cry out, "Mama! Help me! I need you! Where are you? Help me, please, Mama!" Suddenly, out of nowhere, my mother appears. She is standing in the middle of the road, dressed in a wide peasant skirt and a loose-fitting blouse. A scarf covers her satiny, black hair, and she is barefoot. "Hide under my skirt," she whispers. "You are safe now."

I follow her instructions. As I breathe a sigh of relief, I hear the German soldiers stop in front of my mother, still searching for me. They ask if she has seen a girl run past.

"No," my mother tells them firmly.

I woke up drenched in sweat but with a strong sense of inner calm. My mama, my protector, was with me.

There were no swastikas in the Scheibe house, nor were there pictures of the Führer. However, Mr. Scheibe's brother, Robert, was a fervent Nazi. He served in the German army in Warsaw, which was fine with me. He had to travel far to visit, so he came infrequently. He was terrifying. When he visited, the entire tenor of the household changed. He greeted his brother and sister-in-law with the Nazi salute on every possible occasion: when he arrived, when he got up in the morning, when he retired at night, when he left the house, and when he returned.

"Heil Hitler!" he stormed, with his arm projected overhead. Mr. and Mrs. Scheibe answered him uneasily; in this crazy world of the Third Reich, the Nazis had more blood on their hands than in their veins. Many were known to report their own relatives for disloyalty. And yet, I learned that it was Robert Scheibe who had picked me from all the applicants to work on his brother's farm. What an irony! And even meeting me, he did not seem to suspect anything.

—

The real danger for me was still other Poles. I had nothing in common with them, and it was they, much more than the Germans, who endangered my masquerade. Only another Pole could tell one accent from another. Only another Pole could spot an unusual mannerism. Fortunately, I was the only Polish worker on the farm. Unlike the volunteers who worked in German factories, my work was relatively solitary. Had I been surrounded by Poles, I would never have made it. Since my first day on the farm, Mrs. Scheibe had encouraged me to make friends. She told me that there were many Poles working on other farms in Langenwolshendorf. I pretended to be pleased. Many of them were older and had come with families, but there were a few my age, including a young woman named Genka. Mrs. Scheibe encouraged visits by Genka, who came over on some weeknights and every Sunday.

Genka came in her nicest clothes, her round face heavily made up, her shoulder-length hair set and combed in an attempt to give it some life. In her rural Polish dialect, she told me about her adventures and her disappointments, about her typical teenage life. I was happy to keep quiet and listen; when I had to join in, I fabricated stories about myself to keep her amused. Stories about boys, stories about my travels to Warsaw with my father, stories about school—whatever sounded convincing and would not reveal my identity.

Genka invited me to go out dancing or for a beer at the foreigners' tavern and sometimes to visit Kazia and Julianna, two sisters who were too busy with their boyfriends to visit us. She also invited me to go to church, which I did on a couple of occasions. But generally, I pretended not to have finished with my work when Genka came over. I wanted to socialize with the Poles as little as possible, and I was always fearful that Genka would figure out that I was Jewish and report me to the authorities. Fortunately, I was able to keep her at bay. Perhaps she believed that my traditional upbringing made me uncomfortable among the wilder type of Polish girls, many of whom became pregnant out of wedlock.

It was hard to have a perfectly good person whom I might befriend but whom I had to keep at arm's length. I longed for human companionship. At one point, I met a boy in Langenwolshendorf whom I would have liked to know better. He was a loner too. He worked as a blacksmith, fitting horseshoes. He had an intelligent-looking, high forehead, a small, upturned nose, and a thoughtful mouth. The day we met, we spent the whole evening talking together. We spoke about insignificant matters, but I suspected that we had much in common, more than either of us dared to speak. There was no safe way to confirm my suspicion that he was Jewish. All we could do was look into each other's eyes with intense interest, probing for invisible clues. And there was only the one date. Very soon after, he disappeared, and I could not ask about him without endangering myself. A solitary image of him lingers in my mind and I am haunted by the possibility that he thinks I turned him in.

Over time, Mrs. Scheibe began to treat me as a member of the family and was eager to do anything she could, not only for my physical well-being but also for my happiness. Wherever I was when the postman came, in the barn or far off in the field, Mrs. Scheibe found me if there was a letter from my dear friend "Kristina Karmen."

Unlike Kristina, I was cautious about what I wrote in my letters and to whom I sent them. If I could have, I would only have written to her, but it appeared more natural to correspond with many people, so I also wrote to my former neighbors in Warsaw. I reminisced about the time I spent there, sent kisses to the little boy I took care of, and let the baker know I missed the freshly baked bread he used to bring me. I talked about yearning for my Polish motherland, and although I had the same passionate wishes as Kristina, I kept them in my heart and did not write anything bad about the Nazis.

When I would see Mrs. Scheibe riding her bicycle

toward me in the field, her arm outstretched with a white envelope, I would hope it was a letter from Kristina. At the first glimpse of her handwriting, my heart leaped with joy. The great burden of loneliness lifted briefly. I tried never to show too much excitement, but Mrs. Scheibe must have sensed how happy those letters made me. I would accept the letter with a big smile and a silent nod, tuck it into the waist of my peasant skirt, and pray that the day would pass quickly. The letter would always have to wait until I was alone, when I could be sure that no one—especially not my Polish friend Genka—would interrupt me. I could not give her the chance to read over my shoulder; she might have asked questions.

Warsaw
December 22, 1944
Dear Sabina,

As of now, I haven't gotten an answer to the last letter I wrote to you. I cannot understand why you are not writing to me, but I figure that maybe you did not address it right and perhaps it got lost. It often happens this way nowadays. From your last letter to Mrs. Sawicka, I surmised that you are feeling well, and I am very happy about it. My dear, I hope that you will write to me soon and more about your life, because I really want to know how you manage besides the work. My God, when will we ever be able to be together so that we can talk the way we did before?

Dear, I am in the post office and I am writing to you quickly, so you will forgive me for the mistakes

I am making. I took a break from the office so I can write to you. And now you are probably curious about my life. I got a job in an office, and you know this kind of work is not hard for me. But I earn very little and have to look for little things to make extra money just to get by. Besides, I am all alone; my husband went away a few months ago. I was terribly worried and sad for that reason, but it's all in the past now. I'm just existing and just living. Besides that, there is nothing new. I live in a nice room, but I've had enough already. I would like to see all the problems end.

Mrs. Sawicka wants to apologize that she is not writing to you because of her busy schedule. She talks about you very kindly. And she said that her house is always open to you.

I send you kisses and good health.

Love,
Kristina

Rheinhausen 22, Lagenfuhrer
Dear Sabinka,

By chance I found your address on me today, so I am writing to you. I was caught in the uprising of the resistance in Warsaw and have been taken to Germany with the other Poles in the Underground. Below you will find my new address, at a POW camp. The conditions here are terrible. I had to leave everything I had.

I am working as an interpreter for the 350 Poles. Imagine. I am working hard and I like the work I am doing. If you get this letter, please write and tell me how you are, because I want to know. Write lots about everything, and later I will write to you about my life in Germany. Please write a lot about your life. Now we are both in the same boat. I wish you everything good. We are all alone now, just the two of us. We are closer than ever now that we are both in Germany.

I was very upset during the holidays. Now it is New Years, so I am not working in the office, so I am able to write to you. Usually I am in the office all day, until 7 p.m., but I am very happy to be in the office where it is nice and warm.

My lovely child, I wish you everything good and lots of luck in the future, because we have to survive the war.

Hugs and kisses,
Kristina

The last letter I will cherish forever. It was so close to the end of the war.

Rheinhausen, Germany
January 20, 1945
My Dear Little One,

I was very happy when I received your letter. I cannot believe that such a skinny, little girl (in my mind I always think of you as a skinny, little girl) is able to go through life, remove all the obstacles from her path, and manage to go on with life like a heroine and make progress. Dearest, suffering usually makes a person strong. I always knew that you were a fine and gentle girl, and I can't believe you are all grown now. Listen, my little one, write to me more about yourself. I'm counting on you to write about everything.

You probably heard what went on with us in Poland. I went through hell. There are no words for that which I went through, but it is all over now. I was left without anyone or anything, and I am lucky that I survived. The group that I came with are intelligent and elegant people. I met a professor and we talked, because I know German. After I told him about my predicament, he liked me as a very young, intelligent Polish girl. So he said later. I became an interpreter in the place where foreigners reside, like Dutch, Greeks, Belgians, and many other countries.

I am very happy that I am popular, but you know I am altogether different. I am young but have suffered so much in life that I will never forget it; the wounds are so deep that I will never forget my suffering. I pose as a young woman obedient and nice to all the people connected with the position that I have. I have to be polite in spite of my suffering, and that is very important. I feel fine, and I live together in one room with a few people. One is an engineer and his wife, with whom I left Warsaw. Everybody likes me, but nobody knows about my past and what I am going through now.

I'm the only one among five hundred people who has some say. So, dearest, you can see that I don't have an easy job, but I fight back. Besides, I am all alone. I have lost everybody, all the people I loved, and I don't know where anybody is. At this moment, I sincerely believe that I will never be happy again. Everything is already behind me, and I am just trying to push onward. I have to take revenge for the ruined life—that is my goal. And, little one, you write that you don't have anyone left besides me; I too don't have anyone left anymore. I'm happy to tell you, my dear, be happy that you are not alone—that you have a sister, a friend, and maybe even a mother in me. We are lucky that we found each other and we will write to each other as if we are together. So, dearest, that's enough for today. Lots of kisses,

Your sister, as you wish to be called in your letters. We got some news today that perhaps the whole tragic comedy will end soon.

Yours, Kristina

[P.S. Dearest, your boss is addressing your letter to me well.]

I was in the barn the day Genka brought the biggest news I'd had in six years. "The Americans have invaded Germany!" She exclaimed, her blue eyes gleaming. The glow of her happiness was pretty. "This is the end! We can go home!"

Images of home flooded my mind, like newsreels at a movie theater. *Home.* I saw the beautiful hilltop upon which my beloved Serock was perched. I saw the thick, green forests, the raging, blue-green rivers, the newly built school, and the crowded town square. I saw my family's warm, light-filled home. Thinking of my family made my throat constrict and brought me near tears.

Stop. I could not show my feelings. I had to remain calm in front of my Polish friend. I could not show the pain that was bottled up, choking me. I could not reveal my homesickness or my longing. *Keep Bella in check.* I could not even afford one slip of the tongue, one telltale tear.

I knelt and crossed myself, stealing an extra moment

to regain my composure. "Praise the Lord," I said. Genka followed suit.

We stood up and straightened our skirts. My white peasant skirt was prettier than her faded blue one; mine had been a gift from Mrs. Scheibe. I arrived on the farm two years before, at seventeen, wearing a similar skirt, tailor-made for me by my mother. It was already too snug for my developing body, and Mrs. Scheibe had generously replaced it with the blue one.

Genka smoothed her straw-like blond hair and combed her bushy eyebrows with her fingers.

"No more bloodshed," I said. "I've heard that millions of our fellow Polish Catholics have been killed in German work camps."

Genka shook her head sorrowfully.

"And they say that twice as many Jews have been shot or gassed or buried alive," I continued.

"Only twice as many?" asked Genka. "I bet there are still a lot of Jews alive. Too bad the Germans didn't finish the job."

A razor-sharp pain shot through my back at her words, which were now drowned out by the deafening drone of the approaching Allied planes. The loud buzzing was the most magnificent music I had heard since the last time my brothers and I sang in six-part harmony for our parents.

We ran out to the field and saw other foreign workers pouring out of the barns and farmhouses all around. The news had spread in an instant, and celebration was in the air. Everyone was waving at the Allied bombers. We watched as uniformed German soldiers ducked into barns and emerged moments later in civilian clothing.

Cowards, I thought.

Paul, our French prisoner of war, ran toward me, grabbed both my hands in his, and kissed me twice on each cheek. Natalia appeared and gave each of us a big hug, so uncharacteristic for the jealous Russian girl. She had envied my status at the Scheibe farm ever since I'd arrived from Warsaw and was given the spacious, well-furnished room next to the master bedroom. Her turn for the shower was always after mine, and her time off was shorter and less frequent. Even Paul favored me when he had time to lend a hand.

The four of us—Genka, Paul, Natalia, and I—stood together, united in our happiness at the fall of our common enemy. For Paul, Natalia, and Genka, the invasion of the Americans meant freedom from forced labor and the end of a long separation from their loved ones. For me, it meant a vast unknown.

All work stopped. Time stretched and yawned as we watched the planes soar above us. Their gray-white exhaust added pleasing, ephemeral shapes to the sky. In them, I could see the fluffy fleece lining of the embroidered sheepskin coat I once wore, the piles of snow my friends and I had played in, the white cloth on my mother's Sabbath table, and the bushy beard of my grandfather, who looked down at us all from his aristocratic and serene photograph on the wall.

As we stood in the fields, the persistent call of the air-raid sirens accompanied my daydreams like the chords of a pianist accompanying a singer. The blaring notes underscored the melody of liberty and the end of a tragic era. And I had survived to see it all.

I remembered the beginning of the war, when the Germans invaded Poland. I was a child then, a completely different person. Now, more than five years, a lifetime of horrors later, I stared into the sky, mesmerized by the reversal of my fate, the changing world. The Allied planes were coming to redeem the last traces of goodness that had been overlooked by the forces of corruption and doom.

I thought of my dear friend Bella Laska. Was she standing in another field, in another part of Germany, watching the Allied planes? My dear childhood friend, lost and found, and then lost again. In her letters, she had written about wishing for revenge against the Nazis. Putting such things in writing was a dangerous thing to do, but then, so was her becoming a member of the Underground. Had one of her defiant letters to another friend perhaps fallen into the wrong hands? Had her brave but reckless correspondence cost her, her life? I hoped not.

A dog barked, and I realized that I was essentially alone. Paul, Genka, and Natalia were still beside me, but one look at their faces told me that their thoughts were in a different place. They were looking forward to a bright future. I was reviewing my past and had no ideas about my tomorrows. At that moment, if asked, I could not have even stated my own name.

Hours had gone by. The hum of the passing planes rose and fell. Finally the sound disappeared and a powerful silence took over. The stars were out. Ordinarily, we would have finished supper by then. My stomach growled, and I patted it with more than a little embarrassment. Genka gasped a little "oh!" as she woke from her happy trance. She squeezed my hand before taking off toward her farm, right next to ours.

Reluctantly, Paul, Natalia, and I headed toward the dark house. At the door, we were met by Mr. and Mrs. Scheibe, who were returning from the nearby bomb shelter. We studied each other with new eyes. Paul looked taller than usual, and Natalia's cheeks were rosier. I saw new wrinkles on the Scheibes' faces, and their clothes were disheveled. I respected them personally—they had been very good to me—but I was not sorry to see that Germans were finally being humbled.

I thought of one woman, Gizella, one of the local Nazi Youth. I wanted to see her mean spirit broken. Never again would she come in while I was working and taunt me with her supposed German superiority and disdain.

Then I thought of another German girl—Anita, who worked in the fields like all of us. She was probably happy for us. She had never said a mean word to me or any of the other foreigners there. She came and worked with us on the farm, sometimes even without pay, just to keep us company.

With the war ending, the tensions were shifting. The Scheibes were facing collective blame for the actions of their "loyal" relatives and compatriots, like Mr. Scheibe's brother, Robert, the devoted Nazi. From the Allies' perspective, all Germans were the same. The bombers could not have known from the air which homes belonged to Nazi officers and which housed unwilling subjects of the regime.

Mr. Scheibe led the way into the house. Mrs. Scheibe

waved me in ahead of her. I went straight to the kitchen and took five potatoes out of the cupboard. I lit the fire in the stove and filled a pot with water. Except for the rush of the water and the clank of the metal, the house was silent. Paul and Natalia were in their rooms, packing their belongings. We had no idea how long the war would last; they wanted to be ready to leave the moment we got word.

Mr. and Mrs. Scheibe were in the living room, discussing their future. I pretended I did not understand them. As the water came to a boil, I found Mrs. Scheibe at my side.

"Come, Sabina," she said in German. She gestured with her hands as always, to compensate for our language gap. She led me to the living room, where Mr. Scheibe was waiting, pipe in hand.

"Sabina," Mr. Scheibe began stiffly, "we would like you to consider this your home. You may stay here as long as you like. You are like a daughter to us."

This was not the first time the Scheibes had expressed interest in adopting me. The Scheibes may have been rich in property, but they were poor in offspring. Mrs. Scheibe had had several miscarriages while I lived there, and each time I was summoned to comfort her. All I could do was sit beside her in their bedroom, touching her hands, offering silent sympathy.

With the end of the war in sight, the idea of adoption had become a possibility for the Scheibes. Under the Nazi regime, Eastern Europeans had been considered inferior by most of the German population. Adopting a Polish peasant girl would seem as ludicrous as leaving one's estate to a dog or a cat. The Scheibes were either desperate for children, or they had come to truly feel something for me.

That evening, after the Allied planes were long gone from the sky, they escorted me around the huge white house, courting me with their wealth. We walked around the main floor, where they showed me the silverware and fine dishes, the crystal goblets, the linen tablecloths, and the wall tapestries. They led me up the creaky wooden stairs and showed me their feather pillows, down comforters, perfumes, tobacco, soap, and Mrs. Scheibe's fur coats.

Mr. Scheibe lit a kerosene lamp as we walked to the front door. We took a few steps out, and he waved the lamp ceremoniously, as an altar boy waves incense. He motioned toward the row of oak trees, the barn, the stables, the vegetable patch, the orchard, and the vast fields. Then he turned to me and repeated the phrase that I heard after each of Mrs. Scheibe's miscarriages.

"All of this will be yours someday, if you want it."

However much I adjusted to my charade, it was making me sick inside. I'd become a complete stranger to myself, and only in the small moments alone could I even trust myself to think of the joys of my real life and my family. It would have been so easy to say yes to them. They had been kind and supportive. They were a place of stability for me. But listening to them make this offer, I feared drowning.

As good as this simple German couple had been to me, I knew in my heart that becoming their daughter was not an option. These decent people did not know the real Sabina, did not know that I was Bella, once-joyful daughter of two devoted Jewish parents. My life with the Scheibes was a lie. And while I had no idea where I would go or what I would do, I did not believe the Scheibe farm was where I was going to spend the rest of my life. It was not where I, Bella, a Jewish girl from Poland, belonged.

Willy and Lina Scheibe on their farm,
sent to Bella after the war.

Russian soldiers arrived and took control of Langenwolshendorf, replacing the Americans who had been there since the official end of the war. The Americans were a jovial bunch; they passed out cigarettes and chocolates, stockings and food rations. It was they who liberated us, releasing us from bondage, relieving the hunger of many. Before their arrival, hungry foreign workers journeyed regularly from the factories to the farms to beg for food. When I was alone on the farm, I was afraid to give them anything. I welcomed the respite from that source of stress—and the guilt.

The Russians were not as generous; still, workers all over had been freed of our obligations. We were no longer forced into free labor. Paul, Natalia, and I no longer milked the cows, fed the pigs, or weeded the vegetable patch. The corn and wheat would need to be planted soon, and Mr. Scheibe would have to hire many more extra hands from the surrounding villages than before. Most of the young

German men had been conscripted, but there were plenty of women, such as Anita, and older Germans who could use the seasonal income.

The Russians seemed dangerous in ways that the Americans hadn't. One day Natalia and I were wandering around in the backyard, where the season's first fruits were ripening, and through the fence, I saw two Russian soldiers standing in the road. I looked away quickly when I realized they were watching me. Natalia, who was ten years my senior and looks even older in her babushka and peasant dress, noticed them too. I studied her reaction; perhaps she would welcome an opportunity to meet her compatriots. But she showed no sign of feeling any more kinship for them than I did. We succeeded in ignoring them for a few more minutes.

"Hey, miss!" a soldier said, breaking the silence. The other whistled. One would have thought they owned Germany, the way they acted. Their friendliness did not seem genuine.

"Come talk to us!" the first called mockingly.

I looked at Natalia and she looked at me. As if in a choreographed move, we both began moving toward the house. The soldiers persisted. They came through the gate and entered the yard. They moved toward us, talking in Russian. Already they were so close that I could smell the potent garlic and stale sweat that hung in the air around them.

A few of their words were familiar. They seemed to want us to go drinking with them, but it was clear their intentions were not honorable. I shot another glance at Natalia; she was not impressed either. Fear overwhelmed me.

"Paul!" I called out, hoping the wind would carry my voice to Paul's room above the yard. "Paul! Paul!"

Natalia joined in, and our voices were heard. Paul appeared at his window, tall and handsome. His dark features gave him the appearance of a foreign knight. No wonder his girlfriend, Antoinette, willingly waited for him to return to France and marry her.

"Leave them alone!" Paul bellowed at the Russian soldiers in broken German. "Get out of here!" His voice was deeper and louder than I had ever heard it.

The soldiers looked startled. They peered around, trying to identify the source of the command. I grabbed Natalia's hand and pulled her toward the house. The soldiers were too stunned to put up a fight.

I owed a debt of gratitude to Paul. He was always industrious, helpful, refined, and chivalrous.

Not long after, the formal farewells were said, and Paul and Natalia left the farm. I hung back to say one more good-bye to my benevolent bosses. I shook Mr. Scheibe's hand, and he looked away, an agonized expression on his face. I felt a pang of remorse. I thought, *Perhaps I made the wrong decision? Should I stay with them? No. I must move on.*

Mrs. Scheibe took a small package out of her pocket. It was a white handkerchief, the corners tied together, with freshly baked sweet rolls inside. She knew my weakness. I could pass up any of her other delicacies—the sausage made from the blood in the bucket I had to hold under the pig's neck when it was slaughtered; the stews made from the wild rabbits Mr. Scheibe hunted and hung from the

roof; and even potato dumplings, which I helped her prepare, with gravy from the stew—but I never turned down
a sweet roll.

Mrs. Scheibe bit her lip as she handed me the goodies.
I thought of all the things she had done to try to make me
happy: the clothes, the food, the many privileges. I was
leaving with more than I came, in more ways than one.

An image of Mrs. Scheibe bringing me Kristina's letters
crossed my mind, and I bolted up the stairs for one last
look under my pillow to make sure I wasn't leaving any of
those precious letters behind.

On my way back downstairs, I passed a mirror. I
stopped and contemplated my body, bidding farewell to
the awkward girl I had been, getting acquainted with the
mature young woman I was becoming. I finally had blos-
somed into adulthood, as I had seen my friends do earlier,
despite the ravages of war. Starvation, deprivation, horror,
and sheer terror could not keep them from entering the
primes of their lives.

Nature insists on turning ugly duckling teenagers into
beautiful swans under any circumstances. I had watched
the young women dancing in the dirty streets of the ghetto,
holding hands with young men in the dismal stairwells.
Only death itself could stop them.

Springtime had come. It was April 1945. And, seeing
myself in the mirror, I was aware that it was also the spring
of my life.

I walked quickly out the door and headed for the gate
without looking back, fearful that I might change my mind
and stay with the Scheibes. The path to the future was so
uncertain for me; it would surely be easier to remain the

Photo of Bella taken
sometime during the war.

Sabina I had grown accustomed to being. But it was my turn to emerge from my cocoon. The vibrant colors of my newfound wings had to see the sun. In that emotional wasteland, they would only have withered and faded. The time had come to leave my kind hosts and assume my place among the displaced. It was my truth.

• • •

On the main road, I met up with Genka, who appeared elated. We walked toward downtown Langenwolshendorf, to the train depot. We were going to Stuttgart, where we would be processed for redeployment into the shell-shocked world. The train pulled into the station and we climbed aboard, taking two seats next to each other. Genka chattered about the last time she was on a train, when she had come from Poland as a volunteer. She had traveled on a third-class passenger train, much like the one I had traveled on and much like the one we were on now. She had been unsure of where she was going but certain that it was better than starving to death. There had been too many mouths to feed in her family, and the Germans had offered benefits to them all when she'd volunteered to help their cause. After a short stay in Stuttgart, she was going to rejoin her family in Poland.

As the train started to move, I found hot tears streaming from my eyes.

Genka noticed. "You actually will miss them, won't you?"

I nodded, playing into her wrong impression. My tears were not for Mr. and Mrs. Scheibe, but for the thousands of human beings who had been packed into freight cars without food or water and taken their last breaths of putrid air while listening to the sounds of the locomotive.

I spent the duration of the trip feigning attention to Genka's prattle. When we finally descended in Stuttgart, I shielded my bloodshot eyes from the glaring sun and the vibrant colors of spring, and tried to make sense of the scene before me.

"Come on, Sabina!" I heard Genka calling. She was trying to beat the crowd to the processing station.

"Not yet," I told her. "You go on without me."

She looked at me quizzically, then pushed her way into the chaos. Young men and women were hustling about, eager to find a place in a line to somewhere.

There were two throngs. One was vibrant and noisy, like a beehive in springtime. The promise of pollen was in the air, and the worker bees were optimistic, eagerly exchanging information. A hush surrounded the other, smaller group, really a number of solitary individuals around whom sadness hung. I was drawn to them instinctively. Physically, they looked just like all the others. Many looked similar to me with typical Polish features.

Deep, deep in the recesses of my being, I felt a flicker of life as I walked toward the silent survivors. Not one of them moved a limb, but their souls reached out to embrace me like long-lost relatives. We didn't have to say anything to each other. Our eyes met, and we knew.

We had survived.

But I left this group. I was so used to hiding that I wasn't ready to be visible among them. "Wait for me, Genka!" I called, quickening my stride to rejoin her in line.

Genka and I moved with some other Polish girls into a house that had been given to the resettlement movement. The rest of the bureaucratic repatriation process was expected to take longer than anticipated, so we ended up living together in Stuttgart for several weeks. I worked in the group kitchen, preparing meals for the dozens of Polish refugees waiting to go home.

"Sabinka, there is someone here to see you," Genka announced one evening as she rushed into the kitchen. By the singsong quality of her voice, I knew that the visitor was a male.

I left the potatoes I had been peeling in the kitchen sink and dried my hands on a small, spotless towel. At the door to the large kitchen, I saw a young man about my age. His dark hair was slightly unruly, the waves reminiscent of my brothers'.

"Yes?" I asked, wondering why he had singled me out for his attention.

"I am Geniek," he said simply. "I wonder if you would join me for a stroll."

I was a bit flustered by this sudden invitation. Why me? Had I ever seen him before? Had I ever exchanged a word with him? Certainly I had not noticed him. I suspected he lived among the Jewish displaced persons in an area I had passed through but never dallied. Where did he get the nerve to come to the Polish section, to my house, and invite me out for a stroll? And how did he know I am more than just Polish? How could he know? I was put off by my questions. Perhaps I had been Sabina for too long.

"Not right now, thank you," I refused politely. "I have to finish cooking supper."

Geniek mumbled, "Okay," and turned to leave.

He looked so dejected that I felt the urge to lift his spirits. "Maybe some other time," I offered, unintentionally encouraging him to court me.

Over dinner that evening, Genka and my other Polish friends asked me excitedly about the visitor. I changed the subject as quickly as I could. Too many questions.

The following day, Geniek came again to our house. This time it was early afternoon, so we had just finished lunch.

"My sisters and I would like to invite you for supper tonight," he said.

The word "sisters" escaped from my lips, defying my brain's direction. I meant to say, "No, thank you," but the offer was too attractive. He had a family. He was somebody's brother. How I longed to be part of a family again! I could not wait for this processing period to be over, so I could look for my beloved brothers. *Dare I think that perhaps one of them is still alive? Perhaps more than one?*

So I accepted Geniek's invitation. And then another. And another. Over the next few weeks, my stomach was filled with Jewish delicacies at his house five times, and my heart embraced his family of survivors. Geniek and his three sisters were lucky to have found each other after their liberation from different concentration camps. I basked in the warmth of their reunion and shared much with them. Being in their midst redoubled my own strength.

But then Geniek surprised me again. Getting down on his knees in an unexpected gesture of gallantry, he took hold of my quaking hand and told me that finding me had made him feel complete. "In the camps, I never thought I would see this day," he said. "I can hardly believe that I have been blessed with four women to love. When I found each of my sisters, my heart leaped with new life. The moment I saw you, I knew you were my link to the future. Please, Sabina, will you marry me?"

I was overwhelmed. Unprepared. Unable to even grasp his words.

I saw my confusion mirrored in his eyes, which had been so hopeful and optimistic just moments ago. He averted his gaze, only looking back at me after a few seconds. His boldness had melted into embarrassment, his conviction into sadness.

Geniek slumped to the floor as I dropped his hand. My feet carried me back to the street faster than my eyes could adjust to the enveloping darkness. The hot tears stung my cheeks, and I wiped them with the back of my hand. Marry? How could I marry him? I hardly knew him. My heart shattered into shards that pierced my soul. From each hole came the same cry: *Family! You could have had a family!*

I was not ready. I needed to find *my* family.

• • •

Over time, many of the Poles departed, having been given transportation to their various homes throughout Poland. I said my farewells with a mixture of relief, joy, and envy. They were returning to their families.

After nearly a month of waiting, I found myself becoming friends with the Jews. I gravitated to them slowly but was becoming more and more comfortable with them. I began to allow myself the luxury of talking about bits and pieces of my own Jewish heritage. My new Jewish friends talked to me in a mixture of Polish and Yiddish. I understood them, but I answered only in Polish. My mouth was unaccustomed to the language of my youth, though I could still write it. It has been five years since I had lived openly as a Jew, six since I had lived in a Jewish household. I was a child the last time I had sat at a Sabbath dinner table—an impatient child who did not know to treasure the experience.

"Hey, Sabina!" a Polish boy I knew called to me. "What's wrong? Don't you like Poles anymore?"

"Polish or Jewish, it doesn't make any difference to me," I said. That phrase struck me as familiar, and I pondered the context in which I had said it before—it had been a lifetime ago, when I was a girl in school, before being Polish or Jewish really counted.

That childhood was gone completely. I looked behind

me to the past, and I saw a gaping pit. While I had been busy surviving, my youth had fallen into that pit. It had dropped off, lost forever. My unfulfilled dreams and broken connections trailed behind me, weighing me down like a prisoner's ball and chain. I had no idea what to do with myself for the future.

High school was no longer an option; I was too old. I would never have the chance to dance and sing and wear an elegant uniform. I would never be one of those teenage girls whom I used to envy and whom, perhaps, I would envy forever.

My chance to be educated, though, was revived. I heard that the surviving Jews were being offered schooling in the trade of their choice and a card for free passage on the rail lines in order to search for family, in addition to the food, clothing, and lodging provided for them in the displaced persons camp.

I could study and join a profession.

I am alive. I can be of use.

That was what motivated me to come to this office, to the displaced persons camp for Jews.

"So, you understand now," I say, with a great sense of relief. "How I came to seem like a typical Roman Catholic Pole. But I am a Jew."

EPILOGUE

After the War

The story of Sabina came to an end. I felt as if a thousand ears were listening. The DP camp officials were now part of a larger audience. As I spoke, I had seen in their faces a hardness and cynicism that changed at first to interest, and then finally to compassion. The story took far longer than I thought it would, and the sun's rays were beginning to settle for the evening when I finished. I was done with my act. It was the end of the show, *Sabina*. I stood before my audience awaiting approval, a validation more important than applause.

That approval came. I emerged from the office with a new ID showing that I was again Bella Kuligowska. And they let me keep the ID for Sabina Mazurek, a relic of those terrible years that I could not let go of. Like a security blanket, I needed her protection still as I faced the unknown future. I would never know her, but in my heart I offered her my gratitude for saving my life.

• • •

As part of our reentry into the postwar world, the authorities allowed special treatment for the survivors. One benefit was a travel document that allowed me free passage by train to any destination I chose in order to search for my family. My first excursion was back home to Serock. Surely there would be word there of someone who survived.

The train entered the district of Warsaw and the *powiat*, or county, of Pultusk, and I transfered to a bus. We were nearing Serock, and so far the land looked calm and peaceful; it held every bit of the serenity of my memories.

I hurried off the bus in town. I could not wait to retrieve family photographs. We had almost no time to prepare to leave our home, but the one thing I did before they came to evacuate Serock was hide photographs. I remembered collecting them—first the ones Abraham took with his homemade camera: the portrait of me, the photos of my tracks in the snow and of my footprints in the sand. Then, the family pictures. I hoped to find them where I left them: under a little metal roof that shields the back entrance to the basement.

To my amazement, everything looked the same in town. The houses and huts of the Gentiles still dotted the mountain scenery. The apartment buildings and town homes still stood in the most centralized areas, where most of the Jews lived. I ran through the streets and alleyways toward the mountains, toward my beloved, little house. I watched for the familiar horseshoe-shaped sign that always told me I was almost home. Its black letters read *Zaklad Washtatu, Shlusarsko Mechaniczny Calka Kuligowski.* Shop and Workshop, Hardware Mechanic Tzalka (Bezalel) Kuligowski.

But the metal sign, designed by my clever brother Abraham, was gone. As I drew nearer, I realized that not only was the sign missing, but our entire three-room house—stucco, brick, angled roof, and chimney—had been leveled. Big holes were driven into the sleek wooden floor. In the debris, I thought I saw the heavy steel door that once belonged to the oven in our dining room.

I knew I was in the right place. The movie house across the street was still showing films. Our street was a major thoroughfare, once bright, beautiful, and lively. A bus stop was still marked by its sign. Across the street, the home of the janitor who took care of our houses still stood.

The house of one of our neighbors, the old Catholic woman, still stood as well. I used to visit her because she lived alone and welcomed the company. Her dimly lit house, illuminated only by candles, had been cluttered with icons. She usually kept her windows closed, and the air smelled stale and stuffy. Dark tablecloths and covers sheltered her furniture.

Another neighboring family, the Przykorskys, who were also Jewish, were gone, but their home had not been touched. Only three structures were gone: our house in the middle, the Laskas' adjoining on one side, and the two-room building adjoining ours on the other side, which my parents had planned to use to add to our living quarters. They had been negotiating a price with the two sisters who owned it when the war broke out. All three houses were completely dismantled. The stockroom in the back was gone as well. Our stockroom was one of a series of long stalls behind our house, which most people used for horses or other storage. Before we were evacuated from Serock, my brothers and father began digging holes in the floor of our stockroom and burying our valuables there, but they didn't finish in time, and whatever was there was gone now, along with the structures themselves.

My family was uprooted and destroyed. Why had the same happened to my house?

I approached the janitor's home with trepidation. He was gruff fellow, and it turned out, he still lived there. When he opened the door, I asked if he could please help me move aside some of the rubble so I could search for my family's photographs.

"There's nothing left there," he said. His coldness toward me was so intense that I got goose bumps. It was dangerous for surviving Jews to return in Poland. They were not welcome by Poles who appropriated Jewish homes and belongings, and stories of Poles attacking and murdering returning Jews had spread to us in Germany. True, all I came to get were my pictures, but so what? I had no recourse to uncover anything of our former lives; to identify myself publicly as a Jew who had returned to Poland would be suicide. Fortunately, the janitor was occupied with his wife, who lay on a sickbed, needing his attention.

I left hastily, relieved to be away from him. I checked to be sure my Sabina identification was safely in my pocket, grateful to have her still with me.

Dispirited, I went to the first apartment I ever lived in, an efficiency facing Kosciuszko Street. I passed the apartment next to ours, the one once occupied by the Wengers. I couldn't help smiling as I thought of Mrs. Wenger pulling me into her house so many years ago, trying to convince me that I was her son's *besherte*, or destined mate. Mothers have their hopes, their fantasies. Now, my heart went out to her. I had once seen a newspaper clipping about Mrs. Faygele Wenger. It was an eyewitness account of how she had been buried alive. Looking around the area, I realized none of the Jewish families were here anymore. Not one.

I looked for my aunt's hardware store. It stood as it did when we left Serock. Inside, a Polish couple waited on customers. Physically, the *rynek*, town square, had hardly changed, but for me it would never be the same.

My spirits were worn. I ran from place to place, stopping at every house belonging to Jewish families I knew, but there were no signs of them. No one had been back.

I returned to Stuttgart sad and weary. Fortunately, at least my physical needs were cared for. The Allies had forced the Germans to provide us with a place to stay, food to eat, clothing, and other provisions. I lived on the top floor of a two-story house with several other survivors on a quiet, residential street lined with trees and grass.

My next trip was to Biała Podlaska, the last place I saw my parents; my baby brother, Wygdor; and my brothers Joseph and Abraham, and the place where my grandmother and my brother Israel died.

Biała Podlaska looked just as it did the day I left, the day the Jewish work group disappeared. I made my way to the refugee center—there was one set up now in nearly every city—where I joined a few other stragglers in search of familiar names on the lists of survivors. There were none. I added my name to the list: Bella Kuligowska, Fall 1946.

I wandered around, studying what was once my prison. The *volksdeutsch* woman was gone, but I ran into a former neighbor from the ghetto, a Jew who was from Biała Podlaska before the war.

"Your cousin was here," he said.

"My cousin?"

"Yes, Yitzchak Kanier. Isn't he your cousin?"

I was thrilled to hear the name. Yitzchak Kanier was

not a blood relative, but he was married to my first cousin Toba Chmielash.

Toba was the eldest daughter of my father's sister, Golda. My father and his sister had mirror-image families, with Aunt Golda's five daughters and one son corresponding to our family's five sons and one daughter. Her son and I were even in the same class at school.

My aunt had owned a corset shop and made men's underwear. Perhaps as a result of having so many daughters and not enough sons who could work, they were quite poor. When Toba got married, my father gave her a fully stocked notions shop as her dowry; it was one of the shops I would regularly visit as a child.

In fact, Toba and Yitzchak got married in our family's second apartment, the one on Warsaw Street.

I found Yitzchak in a big brick house. His home was warm and inviting, and flavorful food was cooking in the kitchen. Yitzchak told me that Toba was lost, but he survived by hiding in a bunker throughout the war. Then he introduced me to his new wife, who was pregnant. They invited me to stay, but only overnight.

Before I left the next day, I asked about his brother. Back in the ghetto of Biała Podlaska, before I left with the forester, I had noticed him following me around at one point. He was a tall, handsome young man a couple of years my senior. Had his brother found him? Could I see him?

"Come here." Her walk was resolute as Yitzchak's wife lead me into the kitchen where she fingered a hole in the wall. "This is where the bullet stopped after killing him. He committed suicide a few days ago."

• • •

My next trip was to Warsaw. My hope was that someone I knew, perhaps even someone from my family, had passed through the metropolis. I searched the lists at the displaced persons' center, but to no avail. I walked around where the ghetto had been, finding only ruins—broken bricks and torn wooden bits still charred from the burned, empty shells of buildings once packed with my fellow Jews.

As I met the few surviving witnesses and read lists of names—in book form and posted on walls—I found out bits and pieces of information. I asked questions; I searched for anything that might help. I learned from an old neighbor that my sister-in-law, Fela, was shot dead in our apartment the day that I escape from the ghetto in Brześć. Had I not escaped when I did, I would have died there with her.

Always longing deeply for some connection, someone from my past, I found no one close to me, no one to take the place of family or close friends. Even Mrs. Sawicka, who hired me to babysit her son, had disappeared from her apartment on Jaworowska #2.

I gave up on Warsaw. There was no reason for me to stay there, and I had nowhere else in Poland to search for family, so I returned to Stuttgart and began applying for emigration. I joined the throngs of people in line at the central office, where they were registering for work, for trade school, or for visas to go abroad. As some survivors left to take up their futures, others arrived in Stuttgart to take their places.

I considered going to Argentina, where my distant cousins Kalmin and Hinda live. They lived across the street from us on Warsaw Street before going to Argentina in 1938. I remembered my mother giving them a postcard before they left—it was a photograph of my family. I wrote to my cousin Hinda, requesting that she send it to me. "I have nothing, not a single picture," I beseeched her.

She declined. "I do not trust the German mail. Why don't you join us here, so I can deliver it to your hands?"

I considered it, but it was not feasible. Argentina had imposed strict immigration restrictions on Jews, and rumors abounded that they weren't restricting the many Nazis that fled Allied capture. The only way for me to get there would have been by sneaking through Paraguay. I was not ready for another struggle for my life.

Then I remembered that I had two uncles in New York; my father's brothers. I wrote to them, receiving an enthusiastic reply from the older one, who enclosed a photo of himself and his daughter, and a warm reply from the younger uncle. Encouraged, I pushed the application process, completing the paperwork and sitting through interviews.

"Yes," I told the officials, "I am sure I want to go, as long as I know I will be informed if anyone comes looking for me."

What a job it must have been for officials to try and connect survivors with their lost families all over Europe—mostly heartbreaking, though sometimes, perhaps, joyful.

I had one other letter to write. It had been nearly a year since I left the Scheibes, my employers in Germany. It was time now that I was honest with them. I sent my letter and not long after, I got a reply.

Langenwolshendorf
5 March 1946
Dear Sabina,

 We were very happy when we received your letter. We thank you very much. You kept your promise to write to us.

 We heard nothing from Natalia, and we do not have her address. If you hear from her, please send us her address, and I will write to her. We are now occupied by the Russians and have many Russian soldiers here. We can send letters with some of them. She might be very happy. I believe your friend Kristina would also write to you.

 As long as you were with us, we always suspected that you carried a heavy burden in your heart. But we could not figure out what bothered you then. Today we can better understand the heavy burden you carried then. If you had told us everything, we would have never turned you over or told anyone. We would never hurt you. We were always good to each other and satisfied with your work.

 It is a shame we will never be able to make good for the great crime Germany has committed. I was, from the very beginning, against that party. They wanted to arrest me at times for not joining that party. All this was when you were not here yet, when we had all the troubles with that party. Well, you yourself understand.

We are very sorry you did not find members of your family. Perhaps you still will find them later.

We are very sorry that all this happened, and we are concerned about your situation. You went to Warsaw at one time—why didn't you go to Warsaw via Zualenroda? It probably was not a detour. We would have very much liked to talk to you.

Theodor Bei Erz (Lautenschlage) and the Sachs [who worked next door] wrote to us. Genka who worked at Funken has not written yet. On the other hand, the Eismanns already visited for a few days. You can also visit us. You are heartily invited.

We did not get any mail from your friend Kristina. Now, dear Sabina, Bella, I have another favor. In a stormy time of this Russian occupation, where every day they are arresting people, we need a small favor from you: We're sending you a note attesting that we treated you well, which may become important to us. Please sign it or improve upon it, it's up to you. You can send it to us or deliver it in person.

We are very happy that everything is well by you, and we can tell you the same about us. Let us know pretty soon how you are, if you are married and how many children you have and much more. We hope to hear from you soon, and we send our heartfelt greetings.

Willy and Lena Scheibe

I thought well of my employers and of their decent treatment of me and their other workers. They even treated their horses according to the precept of letting all members of one's household, even work animals, rest on the Sabbath.

I answered the Scheibes' request.

LETTER OF RECOMMENDATION

I would like to place into the hands of Willy Scheibe and his wife a few lines of deep appreciation. Although I was born Jewish, I worked for the Scheibe family for two years. My assumed name was Sabina Mazurek, born in Sitnik. At that time, I and my Russian coworker, Natalia Nogeda from Kiev, were treated very well. We were never beaten and food was always good and plentiful. In spite of the laws against such practice, we ate our meals at the family table. If there were any supplements, we always received our share. We were given comfortable sleeping quarters with featherbeds. Willy Scheibe provided us with clothing without rationing stamps. In short, I can only say the best about them. I encourage you to treat this family accordingly.

I sent my letter off but did not receive a reply.

Knock, knock, knock. A persistent, excited beat pounded on my door one morning. I opened it. Had my emigration papers arrived so soon?

"Bella?" I heard in Yiddish. "I have just been to Lodz. There is someone by the name of Kuligowski on the list there."

It's all I needed to hear. I threw some clothes in a bag and boarded the first train. This news offered such hope.

I found the house without much trouble. The door of the Kuligowski home opened; I took one look about me, then broke down and cried. This was not my family.

However, the Kuligowskis in Lodz were very nice to me. They invited me to stay with them for as long as I liked—an invitation from complete strangers that was more generous than my own cousin's husband in Biała Podlaska. So, I decided to stay for just a day or two, to rest between train rides. Then an attractive, blond, blue-eyed man, looking about thirty years old, stepped into the building.

"Bella, meet Herman Zucker." Mr. Kuligowski introduced us in Yiddish. "Herman has been staying next door to us. Herman, this is Bella Kuligowska."

Herman looked at Mr. Kuligowski quizzically, more than a hint of excitement in his eyes. "Your sister? Your cousin? Did you find family?"

"No. No," Mr. Kuligowski said. "Unfortunately, we are of no relation. Just the same name."

"If only we were," I said in Polish.

"You...you don't speak Yiddish?" Herman asked hesitantly, in Yiddish-accented Polish.

"You can speak to me in your *mameh loshon*," I assured him. "I still understand it. I just haven't spoken Yiddish in a long time."

Before I knew it, I was telling him all about my survival under an assumed identity. He seemed genuinely interested, concerned. He asked what it was like.

"I felt like a ghost who had to follow in the shadow of this Christian girl, Sabina. I felt as if I were being pursued by the devil in a game of hide-and-seek. I had to hide myself completely, except in my quiet moments of loneliness. And when I was overtaken by fear or depression, I had to be invisible, even in my own thoughts.

"Some strange power, it seemed, was pushing me, pulling at me, whirling me around in circles—as if the ground were pulled out from under my feet, as if I were spinning in the air without anything of substance to hold on to. I was torn away from reality, from my past. I had no hope for the future nor certainty of my destination."

"I had plenty of time to think during the war," Herman said. "And I also felt that total despair."

Herman explained how he survived—by hiding out for a year and a half in a barn in Silesia. "They cut a space for me to stand." He outlined the four sides of the tiny rectangle with his hand. "I couldn't move around. But at least I could breathe, and I managed to live that way." I looked at him with deep respect. To live that way must have taken an enormous toll on his body and his spirits. Yet we both knew it was better than a camp. If only more Christians had found it in their hearts to hide Jews like that.

We talked about our unsuccessful quests for family members, our future plans, our backgrounds.

"Where are you from?"

I told him about Serock.

"I can't say I have heard of it, but it sounds a lot like my town, Piaski, Lublin." Herman told me about his home, his eight brothers and sisters, and his childhood, which abruptly ended when he was drafted into the Polish army.

"You were discharged around the time that my brother Abraham was drafted." Wistfully, I told Herman about my family. I was so proud of my roots: the love, the successes, the generosity of spirit that surrounded all of us. "My mother could have made us our clothing, but she always bought sweaters for the whole family from a poor girl who needed the income."

Herman nodded in somber admiration.

"Go on," I urged. "Tell me more about your life. What did you do after the army?"

"Well, for the next ten months, until the Germans invaded Poland, I worked as a salesman in my father's grocery store."

"In Serock, we lived right next to a grocery store!" I told

him about the grocer's daughter Bella Laska, my heroine, then as now. "If it hadn't been for the war, she would have had a bright future. Even during the war, she could have gotten away and saved herself. Instead, she stayed near the ghetto. When she had lost everything that was important to her, she kept herself going for one reason: to help her fellow Jews."

I told him about my own escapes from the ghettos and about my final encounter with Bella.

"I was in a ghetto for about the same amount of time as you," Herman said, "from March to October 1941."

"Where were you before that?" I asked, thinking of my family's early deportation from Serock to the ghetto of Biała Podlaska.

Herman told me about the forced labor he endured in Lublin from September 1939 until March 1941. He was removed from the ghetto in the fall of 1941 for more forced labor, this time in Trawnike.

Just like the work group Abraham and Joseph were in when Fela and I were taken to Brześć, just like the poor souls I saw in Biała Podlaska.

A chill ran through me as I imagined Herman and my brothers, all looking like chained shadows, paving roads and digging ditches together.

"My reward for surviving the slave labor was a transfer to a concentration camp," Herman said wryly. "I was there from December 1943 until February 1944. Then I finally had the *chutzpah* to escape. You had a lot more nerve. It was smart of you to take the risk when you still had your health."

"I was just lucky. Remember, I even went back to the ghetto for seconds."

Herman chuckled, and we paused to bask in the warmth of our newfound friendship. He took my hand and I felt a deep joy.

Our conversation continued. I told him how lucky I was that the war ended when it did. "Otherwise, I would have been doomed. Had the war not ended when it did, I seriously doubt I would have survived."

"Why?" Herman asked. "I thought you had perfected your character? Couldn't your show have gone on forever?"

"No. Toward the end, more and more Jewish volunteers were being caught and killed. The Germans were checking documents, looking for imposters. It was only a matter of time before they would have found me."

"Besides," I added, "if Bella Laska did actually keep any of my letters, which I don't know for sure she didn't, the Nazis would have started looking for me when they caught her, which I believe was sometime between January 1945 and the end of the war. Maybe they found my letters; maybe they didn't come after me only because their defeat was imminent and they had to concentrate on staying in the fight. Or maybe they were looking for me and just hadn't the time to catch up."

Herman nodded grimly.

I told him of one memorable scare. It was the winter of 1945, toward the end of the war. I was on my way out of the Scheibes' house one day when suddenly a German soldier sprinted toward me. I tried to remain nonchalant, not to freeze in place. Instead of accosting me, the soldier roughly pushed me aside and ran into the house, straight into the living room. I leaned against the house, holding my breath, certain that he was going to grab me when he emerged. Later, after the soldier had gone, Mrs. Scheibe asked me why I had been so scared. I pretended not to understand her question.

"What was the soldier there for?" asked Herman.

"I never found out," I said. "It would have been risky for me to ask."

Herman agreed. We listened to each other and touched each other and learned to feel deeply comfortable with each other.

Minutes turned to hours. Hours turned into days. And within those days, we felt we knew each other well enough to begin a life—our own new family—together. I had rushed to a strange town to meet strangers whom I believed would be my family, and instead, I made a life connection. We were united in our shared history, in our shared memories of pain and loss, in our pride that we survived, and in hope that a real future would be possible for two survivors who had found each other. We decided to go back to Germany together. We found separate accommodations in the homes of German families in the town of Buchloe, and we began to plan our future together.

• • •

In January 1947, Herman and I put on our best clothes and asked a justice of the peace to marry us. My friend, the only guest, brought homemade cookies. Herman did the photography himself.

None of the pictures came out. If they had, they would

have shown not a vibrant, excited bride, but one who clearly missed her family and couldn't hide it. I was still confused, still heavy with loss and sadness, not ready to be a woman, but too old to be a child. Years of holding back every feeling I ever had now finally took their toll. After the wedding, I sank into depression. Once I had someone to take care of me, once I was safe, I allowed my body to collapse into the exhaustion and heartache I had borne all those lonely years. If I lived, it would be because Herman was kind and was there to care for me. If I died, I wished him well. It hardly made a difference to me. I was numb. Mourning consumed my entire being. After we moved to Stuttgart, I became pregnant, and eventually we bought a small candy store to run. I would find some joy in the challenge of being a businesswoman, but I was always dogged by painful memories and depression.

It was a particularly cold day in the autumn of 1947 when I heard that a group of Polish Jews had come back from Russia—the group my brother Benjamin had traveled with. I last saw Benjamin in September 1939 when he left for Russia with his girlfriend and some other single friends. I had assumed that he, like the rest of my family, had died, but I had not been able to confirm it. Under the leadership of Joseph Stalin and the Soviet party, rumors abounded of how the post-war Russians treated everyone as a spy to be executed immediately. While travel to Poland in search of family had its risks, I had not felt it was safe at all to travel to Russia to search for Benjamin.

But suddenly Benjamin's group was back and traveling just outside Germany, checking lists and signing their names at joint distribution centers that were set up after the war, just like the rest of us had done.

I got the news at work. Excited beyond belief, I pulled on my boots, wrapped my coat around my pregnant belly, grabbed some money for travel, and abandoned my post at the counter, leaving Herman to work the store.

The train ride was long; I had to ride all the way to Gdansk, on the farthest end of Poland, to find them. Between the distance and my anxiety, by the time I arrived, I was totally exhausted. Still I climbed off the train quickly, careful not to fall. I had to get to Benjamin as fast as I could.

Benjamin, Benjamin, Benjamin! My brother, my companion, my dance partner, my closest sibling, my look-alike.

I was greeted enthusiastically by various members of his group. I embraced them quickly, named them as much as I could remember, touched a few with my greeting, but kept my eyes out for Benjamin. *Where was he?*

I spotted his girlfriend, Edgia. She was holding a baby. *A precious baby. Benjamin's child!*

I ran to her and hugged her, kissing her baby wildly. "Can I hold him?" I was anxious for contact with my nephew, my own flesh and blood.

"Sure," she said, handing him to me, but her eyes dropped, and she didn't look at me.

I cooed at the baby and coddled him in my arms. "Where's Benjamin?"

Silence, as deafening as the roar of a thousand bombers.

"What is it?" I asked, my voice cracking, reaching an unnaturally high pitch. "Where is he?" But I knew the answer before she opened her mouth.

"Oh," she mumbled self-consciously, eyeing her baby. "Oh, no. Oh, Bella. Oh, no."

"Oh, no," I echoed. I looked at the baby. "Benjamin's?" I asked, not wanting to know.

She shook her head sadly. "Benjamin supported us

196

all for a while. You know, he was such an amazing businessman. Just like your whole family, he was able to make enough money to feed us all. Then, when the Russians entered the war, he enlisted. I begged him not to leave me and our group, but he insisted. He actually believed his family's welfare and the future of the Jewish people depended on his ability to enter the battle. He got killed fighting the Nazis."

I handed her back her child, then turned away, telling myself I had no right to be angry. *It was not her fault that he died. It was not her fault that she married someone else after Benjamin died. It was not her fault that I had no family.*

I stood there, avoiding eye contact. I was crushed. A wave of utter exhaustion swept over me. A few of Benjamin's friends lightly touched my shoulder or my arm, their hands expressing what their words could not.

• • •

Helen was born on November 12, 1947, in Stuttgart. While I smiled for her, I still could not smile for myself. My world was still upside down. It seemed that I had more luck during the war than after. Except for this blessed baby and her beautiful little face, nothing felt right.

Helen was named after my mother, Chaya, and Herman's mother, Feige. I had no mother to show me how to feed a baby, no sisters-in-law to show me how to bathe her, no cousins to bring little gifts, and no friends anxious to hold her. As a child, I never imagined I would be alone for these sorts of adult milestones. Despite my joy at being a mother, I barely had enough energy to get out of bed in the morning.

All the Jewish survivors were busy fending for themselves. Everyone was trying to put the pieces of our lives back together, to renew our lost worlds, but it meant that friends were almost as hard to come by as relatives.

• • •

A surprise visitor revitalized me. Morris Wenger, my former classmate, the boy next door whose mother had wanted me for a daughter-in-law, arrived with his wife, Sara, and their daughter, Fay.

Morris and I touched each other often and with affection, verifying that we were really sitting before each other. We recounted the cheerful days of our youth, and then shared our own stories about the horrors of the war.

I thought back to our childhood. "Before the Germans invaded, I don't even remember anti-Semitism," I commented. "We all lived together in the community as good neighbors. The Jewish and non-Jewish children in school got along fine too, just like the adults."

"It was there," Morris said. "Don't you remember the schoolyard scuffles?"

"I guess I remember the words 'dirty Jew' being used sometimes when we split up for religious services on national holidays, though I never personally witnessed any fighting." I considered it longer. "I'm sure my parents knew of anti-Semitic outbreaks, but they never told me about them. I was the little princess of the family, so I was often sheltered. It was that way before the war and even during the

לשנה טובה תכתבו
Our best wishes to New-Year.

תש-ט

Bella, Herman and Helen on a
Jewish New Year card, dated fall 1948.

first calamities that befell us. Sure, I heard about pogroms in other towns, but to me it seemed unreal, distant. I also heard that there was discrimination in the universities, but I was too young to understand its significance."

Morris shook his head, incredulous at my naiveté. "Didn't you think there was something strange behind the total indifference the Gentiles showed when we were oppressed and degraded over and over again? Didn't you know that most of your father's profits went to the Polish government in the form of special taxes for Jewish businesses?"

Perhaps I had chosen not to know. I had played the innocent. Looking back now, I could see the value of this denial. My memories of early childhood were, indeed, idealized. I had painted a picture so perfect, so serene, so loving and supportive, and those memories had sustained me in my bleakest moments.

Morris and I kept our promise to stay in touch. So few of our townspeople, our *landsmen*, were alive, and I wanted to be certain that I did not lose track of this dear childhood friend.

Shortly after I reconnected with Morris Wenger, Herman got the most wonderful news. His older brother, Moishe was alive! He and his wife, Fruma, had moved to Stuttgart and found Herman by going to the displaced persons center. They survived the war nearly the same way that Morris Wenger did: by escaping to Russia and staying out of the Nazis' path.

With them were their daughters, Fraidele and Gittel, who were born before the war, and their son, Mendel, born in Russia.

Herman and Moishe hatched a plan for the future. We would all make *aliyah* and move to Israel. Moishe, who was an experienced baker, would lead the way with his family and would establish a bakery in Israel. Herman and I agreed to invest all of our savings in the venture: we paid for state-of-the-art refrigerators, commercial stoves, and other bakery equipment. Once the business had been established, Herman and I would join Moishe and his family, and we would be partners in the business—in the Jewish homeland.

The prospect of Israel was very inviting. From an early age, my brothers and I were taught that Israel is the birthplace of the Jewish nation and the ultimate homeland for the Jews. Our nation had taken root there once again, and I was anxious to be a part of the Zionist movement, whose flag my brothers had proudly bore. There was nothing that would make my brothers more proud of me than moving to Israel.

We waited what felt like forever for a letter from Moishe and Fruma, the one that would tell us it was time to pack up our baby and our belongings and join them in Israel.

At long last, in the fall of 1949, a letter arrived. I left Helen with the nursemaid and rushed the thin airmail paper, still folded and sealed, to Herman at the store. Hope provided a surge of energy for me, and my frail body moved faster than it had since before childbirth.

Herman opened the letter and read aloud in Yiddish.

Dear Herman and Bella,

I had hoped to write that our bakery is running and there is enough business to support us all. Man plans and God laughs.

You would not believe what it is like here. We (the immigrants) have been assigned to tents. That would not be so bad if only our belongings were placed in decent storage. I have just come back from the tent that is housing all our precious equipment and the ovens and refrigerators that we bought with the money earned through our sweat and tears. It breaks my heart to report this, but I must. Please do not blame the messenger for the message. I did everything in my power to get the officials here to move the equipment indoors.

It has all been rained on. The electrical circuits are ruined. The metal is rusting. The machines are useless. Our dreams of a modern, automated bakery are gone. I am so sorry, so very sorry for you, for your family, for us.

I will seek work as a baker in someone else's bakery and will write to you again as soon as I have myself and my family somewhat taken care of. We will make whatever sacrifices are necessary to help get you established here with us.

Moishe and Fruma

Herman and I were heartbroken; Israel had lost its allure. It was not an option to move there if the government was unable to effectively integrate the brave immigrants who had survived this war. In a way, it would have been easy enough for us to stay in Germany. After the war, the Allies became a forceful presence in the country. Germans were scared; some felt guilty, especially those who knew they might have spoken out, might have saved a life or a family. The Allies forced the Germans to evacuate their own homes and gave those homes over to any surviving Jews. If the Germans hated us, it didn't matter. They were now an occupied people.

Yet, in Germany, I continued to be preoccupied by the

fruitless search for my family. It was a fixation I could not let go, and I would stare at the few pictures I had of them. I was simply not at peace, not when I continued to mourn them so much that I was unable to function emotionally.

Herman and I went to the office of the Hebrew Immigrant Aid Society with our precious two-year-old daughter, Helen, and our identification documents. We waited in line, filled out papers, and answered questions.

"America," we said in unison. "Yes, we're sure."

Before long, the letter from HIAS arrived with instructions. We followed them and boarded the ship in Bremerhaven, Germany for our travel to America. We arrived in New York City on February 19, 1950. Unfortunately, both of my uncles had passed away since my previous correspondence with them, and I did not find a connection with their surviving families. Instead, we followed the HIAS assignment to Rock Island, Illinois, where we started off sharing a house with another family and were supplied with rent, food, and medical care. We got jobs, learned English, and moved to Chicago. Eventually, we had a second daughter, Grace. We went on and built our lives. But we made sure to raise our daughters with *yiddishkeit*; we wanted them to know their heritage.

I t was 1960, when I thought again of the Scheibes. I dug out the last letter I received in 1946, when they had asked for my recommendation regarding their good behavior toward their employees during the war. They were true friends to me; they did not question me when I needed to not be questioned. And they invited me to rejoin them, without prejudice, when I told them who I really was.

I decided to renew contact, and I have just a few letters from Mrs. Scheibe still that I keep close.

> *Dear Family Scheibe,*
>
> *You have probably already forgotten me. I am Bella Kuligowska, better known to you both as Sabina Mazurek. Now for the last thirteen years, I have been Bella Zucker. I am married and have children. Both are girls. One is twelve years old and*

is already as tall as I am. The other is sixteen months old and is also a fine child.

Very often I think about you. Many times I wanted to write to you, but I did not get an answer to the last letter that I sent you many years ago. In it was the note you sent for me to sign. In that note it was written that I was treated well by you during the war. I thought maybe you didn't want to be in contact with me anymore. But then I also thought that your letter or mine got lost. That is why I am writing to you.

I have been many places during the past years. I came to America from Stuttgart, Germany, in 1950, where I lived after the war. I love this country very much. I have a nice home now and a nice family. We live in Chicago.

I never found any of my five brothers or my parents. I never found any relatives of mine at all. I am the only survivor of my entire family. If the war would have lasted any longer, I don't think I would be alive today.

I saved all my documents and the letters I got from Kristina. She was also a Jewish girl. She lived next door to us before the war and was my very dear friend. Just before I went to Germany to work, I met her on the street in Warsaw by sheer accident. Ever since, we kept in touch with each other. We were risking both our lives doing so, but our need for communication was so great, we had to take that chance.

After the war was over, I hoped to meet Kristina and never part again, but I never heard from her.

Maybe she has gotten in touch with you? It is my deep hope. If so, please let me know.

I would like to know how all of you are, because I will never forget you. You really treated me like your own child. I was very lucky to have come to you to work. I liked you very much and still do.

I don't blame you for what happened. I only wish I could have told you what was bothering me for so many years.

I hope we will always be in contact with each other from now on.

Yours,
Bella

Langenwolshendorf
January 29, 1960
Dear Mrs. Bella Zucker,

I was very surprised when I got a letter from America under the name of Bella, and I understand that it was our Sabina. You cannot believe how very happy I was that you did not forget us. We often spoke about you. When we got your letter, we wrote back to you, but the address was Buchloe in Schwaben. We wonder if you heard from Kristina? Now we can understand why you openly cried, and we felt sorry for you but did not understand why you were crying.

Now I will tell you a little about us. On January 27, 1952, my brother-in-law, Robert Scheibe, the one who visited us, died. On the 16th of May 1952, my dear husband, you may still remember he loved the forest and the farm, killed himself and closed his eyes forever. At that time, I was away in Zeulenroda, and when I came back to the house, I found him dead. What a state I was in, I cannot describe.

In 1946, we adopted a three-year-old girl, Marlies, who is seventeen now. You cannot imagine what I went through the past eight years. The two horses we had when you were with us are now dead. There was another eight-year-old horse that had to be destroyed by stabbing. Then I bought another horse, and then I had four cows get sick. I did not get any money for any of the losses. And you remember how big our farm was. I cannot do anything but work and worry about the future. I hope that Marlies will find a man to marry soon and things will get better again soon.

I am glad that you are married and that you have a lovely family. Please send me another picture, and I will be happy with it. Also, I will be happy if you can come to visit me in Germany, because we have a lot to talk about, also I don't have anyone to translate your letters. I wish you lots of luck and all the best. And write again really soon.

With love,

Yours,
Lene Scheibe

February 8, 1960
Dear Mrs. Scheibe and Daughter:
I received your letter for which I thank you very much. But I could not honestly say that the things you had to tell me were very good. I am very sorry

that your loving husband died so young, and that you had to take over the responsibility of managing the big farm. I know from before how happy you were together, and I loved you both very much.

I can imagine what you went through after the war, for all of the change came very suddenly. All of the help that you had left you very suddenly and at the same time. What was worse, they left all the work that had to be done right away. I assume it was hard to get someone to work at a time of great confusion, as it was at that time.

I am very sorry that I did not stay, but you must know how I felt at that time. I think I must have been the most confused girl on earth. I know now that if the Russian troops would not have taken over the territory, I would have come back to you, to stay at least until I knew what to do with myself. At the time, I did not have any place to go, or anyone that I knew.

I found myself in a world completely strange to me. I did not know whether I should be happy or sad. Yes, I had freedom, and all of a sudden, many roads opened before me, but I did not know which way to go.

As a result, I could not come to you for a long time. I was in a great state of shock and depression, and as if completely blindfolded, I could not recognize or adequately respond to the real world. I lived in a world of darkness, still scared to admit the truth to others.

Maybe if I had been able to find someone close to me, I would have awakened sooner. I lived in a world

*of deception and avoidance. But to my great confu-
sion, I did not find anybody close enough to trust.*

*I met my husband in the endless search for my
family in Poland. We got married soon after we met.
My husband also lost his entire family, except for one
older brother. He now lives in Israel with his family.*

*My husband, unlike myself, did not have the
freedom I enjoyed with you. I had the open air and
the growing fields. He was in a hideout on a farm
in Poland. The place was made for him in a barn,
where he could only sit, stand, or lie down, with his
legs always bent. It was not big enough to move in,
to stretch out, or catch some fresh air. As a result, he
became very nervous and distressed.*

*As for the rest of my family, the children are well.
Our older daughter is in the seventh grade in public
school and is a very good student. The little one seems
to be a fine child also. My husband is in the real estate
business now. I worked with him earlier in a store,
and now I am a housewife. I am sending you a picture, which is not the latest, but as soon as we make
another picture, I will send it to you immediately.*

*Now I would like to know a little more about
how you are managing your farm and who is helping
you in the fields and if you have any modern equipment in the house or in the fields. I mean things like
a washing machine, refrigerator, or maybe a tractor.
All this would help you and make it easier for you.*

*Someday, I would like see how life is on a farm in
America. Then I would write you all about it.*

Oh, I have so much to tell you, but right now all

my thoughts are mixed up, so I will write more in my next letter. Please call me "Bella," instead of "Mrs." Thank you.

Remember that I will never forget you and your kindness toward me, for you tried to make me feel at home while I was in your house.

I am very sorry that Mr. Scheibe could not share these letters with you, because I know how much he wanted to know that I was pleased and comfortable in his house.

Also, please do not worry too much, for better times will come. I hope.

Please write how you and your husband felt about me while I stayed with you and what all my friends said after you told them I was Bella, not Sabina.

Everybody was so good to me. I still remember Anita, Gisela, and many others whose names I forget already. But I will be very happy if you will write and let me know how everybody is. They may also write to me personally.

Please give everybody my regards.

Have you heard anything from Paul? He also was a fine man. I wonder if he is thinking about me sometimes, but that is not important.

I hope everything will work out fine for you and everyone concerned.

Please write again real soon, for I am happy to hear from you.

Thank you very much, with love always,

Yours,
Bella

Lg. Wolshendorf
May 8, 1960
Dear Bella,

I think the time has finally come that I have to thank you for your letter and for that wonderful picture, but you must forgive me because I have been sick and had much work. I want to refer once more to the picture, which shows a really beautiful family, and both girls are very beautiful—the little one looks like the mother and the big one looks like the father. From their total appearance, it looks like things are going well for them.

I can believe that you were depressed at times, since you were alone in a strange environment and had nobody to trust. I can really understand how your dear husband could not endure being in such a small place. That he was uncomfortable is no wonder.

Now you, no doubt, want to know who does the work in the fields. The preparation of the fields, the hoeing and the seeding, and the mowing of the grass is done by MTS farming cooperative, but the maintenance and the harvesting we do ourselves. Bringing everything into the barn was done with the help of one horse. One cannot get workers and also it would be difficult for me to pay them. I can only afford to pay the MTS, and there is little left for me.

You cannot imagine how the situation is over here. I would really like to "unload my heart" for you, but I cannot do this. You will, no doubt, understand. The new things that they have introduced are great, and I would like to have them, but I cannot afford them.

My husband and I often said that you were courageous to go to a foreign country under a false name. One can only wish you the best of congratulations in your accomplishments. Otherwise you might not be alive today. All our friends said the same thing, and they are always very happy when I receive mail from you. They also admired the picture that you sent. Perhaps you will remember Erz, Funke, and Lautenschlaegen. Anita got married in West Germany, and I don't know what became of Gisela. We also never heard from Paul.

Dear Bella, you don't realize how much I appreciate it that you have not forgotten me, and how much I wish that we could converse with each other. Please write to me again soon.

Lena Scheibe

Lg. Wolshendorf
Sept. 6, 1960
Dear Bella,

I just wanted to ask whether you received my letter, in which I thanked you for the picture. I have been waiting a long time for news from you.

There is much work to be done here with the grain harvest, with which we are now finished. Now comes the hoeing if only the weather holds out. At the moment it is very cold.

How are you doing? I hope well.

With best greetings, I remain truly,

Lene Scheibe
P.S. Greetings from Ms. Jaeger. I hope for a prompt reply.

September 14, 1960
Dear Mrs. Scheibe:

I thank you very much for your letter and your lovely card. I'm very sorry that I didn't write earlier. I found time was slipping away from me so quickly. I'm very happy that everything is fine with you and that you manage to do the work on your farm. Everything is okay here. The children are fine.

Your kindness while I was with you was payment enough for me. Money cannot ever pay for your loving help and care, and if it could, it would be the other way around—that I would owe you money, instead. It is true that it was hard for me to keep that secret to myself, and I felt many times like telling you the whole truth and yet I had to keep it. I'm very glad you were so considerate in not asking any questions at that time. My hardest trouble was finding enough work to do to occupy my mind, helping me forget the truth and the homesickness I felt. Anyway, I'm glad it's all over and that I don't have to live in fear anymore, and I'm trying to write everything, all my feelings, all my fears, in a book which I'll send you as soon as it is completed so you will understand why I did all the things I did. About you I have only to say good things because you really helped in my survival. My life was in your hands, and I thank you for taking care of it as if it were your own.

In helping to straighten out a few things that might be troubling you about myself, the documents I carried under the name of Sabina showed the age as being five years older than I really was. It was hard to hide those extra five years and keep the truth from you. Now those five years have caught up with me, but thank heaven they don't show fear and depression, as they would have if I would have stayed there.

I'm very happy that all the neighbors remember me. My family and I send them our best regards. God bless them all and may they prosper and be in good health. Otherwise, I don't have anything to write except that we are all well. My older daughter will be thirteen years old and in the eighth grade of public school, and the little one is two years old and also a fine girl.

I would like you to send some pictures of yourself and your daughter. Please write soon and tell me what you have been doing and how you are getting along.

With deepest regards,
Bella

Bella and her two daughters,
Helen and Grace, taken in 2000.

I never gave up looking for our lost family and friends. Herman and I added their names to the memorials at Yad Vashem in Jerusalem and at the United States Holocaust Memorial Museum in Washington, DC. I sat for an interview with Steven Spielberg's Shoah Foundation to be placed in their Visual History Archive. Herman served on a committee of Holocaust survivors that the mayor of Skokie organized to help craft the city's response when the National Socialist Party of America wanted to march in Skokie, Illinois, in 1977. We also donated our original documents and photographs to the United States Holocaust Memorial Museum and the Illinois Holocaust Museum and Education Center in Skokie.

In America, my husband and I found success and a measure of safety and security. We built businesses, raised our girls, and traveled. We moved forward, always hoping for better times. We *lived*.

But I never felt far from the war, from the deprivation,

danger, and loss. I always felt that I was still surviving the deaths of so many people I knew and loved. I was never able to completely escape the Holocaust.

We must never forget.

For Mama, Papa, and my brothers. I miss you.

Bella visited Serock in 1998. She is standing in front of a sign as she enters her town for the first time in 60 years.

SEROCK

Bella Kuligowska Zucker

I remember the steep hills
And life on its peaks
I remember the valleys
Where the rivers flow
The brooks and the meadows
All full of life, the forests, its sounds

But most of all, my little town
Where I was born and raised
With my family, my friends
Suddenly, like a black cloud, up high
Gray planes appeared in the sky
In horror, in fear, I see destruction
And death everywhere.

Where have you all gone, fantasies, my dreams?
Happiness, are you playing tricks on me?
Are you sinking into quicksand
While the earth goes up in flames?

When the storm had past
I, a wanderer in a daze
Asking these questions
Over and over again

Where is my mother?
Where is my father? My brothers?
My uncles, my aunts?
My cousins, my friends?

Where are their graves?
Maybe the gas chambers were destined for them
In a pit, or in the belly of the beast
In the ashes, piled high
Or just maybe, buried alive?

How can it be?
Why was it allowed
For someone to choose
Who lives or who dies?

I, just I, was spared
To wonder, to tell
Never to forget
The horrors of Hell

I am deeply grateful to this book's editor, Jaime Levine, who provided the exceptional editorial skills, lovingly administered, that were needed to finally get this book published. Jaime became my partner and a friend – treating this project with such loving care, you wouldn't believe that Bella wasn't a member of her family too. She ensured that we preserved Bella's original manuscript and logged in many hours, over and above what was required, to make sure every detail is true to Bella's story and is portrayed as accurately as possible. She tested concepts and interest in the book with friends in the industry, and worked with me to prepare promotional pitches and outreach that resulted in the manuscript being read by several significant publishers and agents. She marshaled her personal and professional network to get the translations done, the copy edited, and the book cover design and formatting finished. This book would never have seen the light of day without her.

I also want to give thanks to Miriam Aronin, who worked with me as an editor in the early days of this project to create a manuscript that we used to pitch the book to young adult publishers.

I am grateful for the assistance of my nephew, David Neuman, who has always been interested in his grandmother's story. Even before we started working together to get the book published, David was sharing the manuscript with his friends and talking about and teaching from Bella's experiences. It was a treat to work with him on pulling together some of the major pieces of this book. Thanks also to my nephew Daniel Neuman, who is our Israel-based connection to Yad Vashem in Jerusalem and their memoir publishing branch.

Two devoted high school teachers validated for us the necessity of making Bella's story available as a young adult book. We are so grateful to Amadis Raul Velez in San Francisco and Jennifer Snow Loder in Newfoundland, Canada, who have used Bella's manuscript as a supplement to their lesson plans about the Holocaust and invited both David and me to talk to their classes about Bella's experiences. The students shared their profound reactions to this material and we were convinced that Bella's story has resonance with young adults as a universal story about resilience and survival and can serve as a roadmap about how to carry on when all else has been lost.

Original artifacts and papers, including Sabina's identity card, letters and photographs, are now part of the archives at the US Holocaust Memorial Museum in Washington, DC and the Illinois Holocaust Museum and Education Center in Skokie, Illinois. Thanks to Curator

Susan Goldstein Snyder, who worked with Bella directly to donate these items to the US Holocaust Memorial Museum's collection and provided digitized images of the documents included in this book. Thanks also to Emily Mohney – Registrar at the Illinois Holocaust Museum and Education Center, Skokie, Illinois, who digitized and shared documents now in the Illinois museum's collection. And a thank you to Stacey Saiontz, Next Generation Board of the US Holocaust Memorial Museum.

Many translators in a variety of languages were needed to understand and interpret the letters and documents in Bella's story. Many thanks to all of these people, who contributed their time and expertise to this book:

Mateusz Kopytra – Polish translations
Jolanta and Carolyn Geisel – Polish translations
Jack Grossman – Yiddish translations
Aleks Gonschewski – German translations

Warm thanks to Gretchen Stelter, who completed the copy-editing but also provided a fresh set of eyes and questioned us when elements of the book were too opaque or didn't make sense to a non-Jewish reader. Sarah Masterson Hally pitched in on all of the final necessities – the cover design, formatting, and cataloguing of the book – prepping it for its long awaited debut.

And a shout-out to my husband Bruce Rapkin, who has been hearing about this book since the day he met me and pitched in in numerous, uncountable ways to make sure I had what I needed to get this project done.

With gratitude to all, this is a most fitting memorial to

our beloved mother and grandmother Bella, on behalf of myself and my sister Helen Zucker Stolar.

Grace Zucker Rapkin

BELLA KULIGOWSKA ZUCKER was born in Serock, Poland in 1925. She was a teenager when she was separated from her home and family and found herself completely alone in a time of great peril. After the war, she moved to Chicago, Illinois, and spent her life dedicated to writing this memoir of her experiences during the Holocaust.

Since this book was a lifelong project of Bella's, we have preserved her voice and original manuscript with minimal editing for accuracy, spelling and grammar only. We have tried to be true to the actual Polish and German names of places mentioned in the book. Langenwolshendorf, Germany, where the Scheibe farm was located is a municipality in the district of Greiz, in Thuringia, Germany and is located about 500 miles from Warsaw.

APPENDIX

Droga Sabinko!

Napisałam w swoim czasie list do Ciebie nie dostałam natomiast odpowiedzi, byłam bardzo zmartwiona, gdyż naprawdę nie mogłam zrozumieć dlaczego do mnie nie piszesz, ale teraz tłumaczę sobie tem, że może być, że adresowany i nie doszedł zresztą to się często zdarza.

Z ostatniego listu do p. Świrskiej, wywnioskowałam że dobrze się czujesz, i że ~~...~~ jestem z tego bardzo zadowolona. Moja droga mam nadzieję, że do mnie napiszesz więcej o swoim życiu, jestem naprawdę ciekawa jak sobie prócz pracy radzisz i żyjesz.

Mój Boże kiedyż to będziemy mogli być razem, żeby trochę porozmawiać tak jak to kiedyś było. Kochana jestem na poczcie i piszę na poczekaniu, tak że wybaczysz mi pewne niedokładności jakie tu robię, zwolniłam się specjalnie z biura żeby napisać do Ciebie. A teraz jesteś chyba

Letter to Sabina from Kristina Karmen (page 1).
No date. In Polish.

ciekawe jak ja żyję. Dostałem posadę
w biurze, pracuję, wiesz biurowa praca jest
dla mnie nie trudna, ale bardzo mało
zarabiam, muszę dopiero coś kombinować
żeby starczyło na życie, poza tym jestem
sama, mąż mój wyjechał kilka miesięcy
temu, byłam strasznie zmartwiona i zrozpa-
czona z tego powodu, ale to już poszło
żyje się poprostu z przyzwyczajenia jak
ja mówię, ale się żyje. Poza tym
u mnie nic nowego. Poślij anonn
ładny, gdyż niedawno się przeprowadziłam
ale już mam dość. Chciałabym żeby
się to wszystko skończyło. P. Sawicka
b. Cię przeprasza, że nie pisze ale ona
nie ma czasu, bardzo serdecznie o tobie
się wyraża i twierdzi, że jej dom
jest dla Ciebie otwarty zawsze.
    No całuję Cię mocno i pozdrawiam
    Serdecznie Krystyna.

Letter to Sabina from Kristina Karmen (page 2).
No date. In Polish.

Langenwolschendorf, den 5 März 1946.

Liebe Bella!

Wie freuen wir uns als wir Deinen Brief erhielten und danken
Dir recht herzlich dafür. Hast also doch Dein Versprechen gehalten.
Natalia hat noch nicht hören lassen. Auch habe ich von ihr keine
Adresse. Wenn Du noch die Anschrift weist dann schreibe mir das nächste
mal mit. Wir haben hier viele rus. Soldaten wo ich einen Brief mitgeben
könnte. Sie würde sich sicher freuen. Ich glaube Ihre Schwester Würde
auch wieder schreiben.
Solang Du bei uns warst merkten wir immer, dass Du etwas auf den Herzen
hast konnten aber nicht dahinter kommen. Heute können wir Dein Schluch
desto besser verstehen. Wenn Du uns seinerzeit dies erzählt hättest ich
hätte Dich nie verraten. Warum den auch wir waren doch immer gut zu ei-
nanter und mit der Arbeit zufrieden. Es ist eine grosse Schande, die nie
wieder gut zu machen ist, das solche grosse Verbrecher Deutschland führte
Ich war ja von allen Anfang gegner dieser Partei mann wollte mich ja auch
mal verhaften wo Du noch nicht da warst. Was hatte ich mit Helbig alles
für Schererei der auch nicht mer da ist Nun Du weist ja selbst doch
noch alles. Wir bedauern sehr, dass Du von Deinen Verwanden keins mehr
vorgefunden hast. Vieleicht findest Du doch noch später von Deinen
Angehörigen jmand. Die Welt ist doch noch ganz durcheinanter
Warum bist Du den nicht über Zeulenroda gefahren wie Du in Warschau
warst. Esist doch bestimmt kein Umweg gewesen. Wir hätten gern mit Dir
mal gesprochen.
Teodor Bei Erz(Lautenschlägern), Michel beiLautners und der bei Sachs
haben geschrieben. Genga und di bei Funken noch nicht. Dagegen der bei
Eismanns war schon da zu besuch auf einige Tage. Also Du kannst uns
auch mal besuchen bist herzlich eingeladen.
Das Wobst Gut Ist an 6 kleine Bauern aufgeteilt
Wir haben uns wir .... genommen wo die Mutter auf der Flucht
gestorben ist und der Vater ver .... d. Unser kleine Marilen weil
jetzt 3 Jahre.
Von Deiner Freundin Christina Kurmann haben wir keine Post erhalten.
Nun liebe Sabine, Bella hätte ich noch eine Bitte. In dieser bewegten
Zeit, wo man jeden Tag verhaftet werden kann wegen irgend einer kleinen
Sache, könntest Du mir eine Bescheinigung schreiben, die mir vieleicht
mal vom Wert sein kann. Ich lege Dir es bei und Du kannst es unter-
schreiben oder umbessern wie Du es willst. Oder bringe es bei Deinen
besuch mit.
Wir freuen uns, dasses Dir noch gut geht und können dasselbe auch von
uns schreiben.
Lass recht bald von Dir hören, vor allen was Du machst ob Du verheirat
bist wieviel Kinder und dergleichen mehr.

Wir hoffen recht bald von Dir zu hören und grüssen
dich recht herzlich

Willy Scheibe Frau

Letter from the Scheibes to Bella dated March 5, 1946.
In German.

Aus Dankbarkeit möchte ich Willy Scheibe & Frau von
Langenwolschendorf einige Zeilen in die Hand geben

Bei der Familie Scheibe war ich 2 Jahre unter falschen
Namen tätig und bin eine geb. Jüdin. Mein falscher Name war
Sabine Mazurek geb. in Warschau. Wärend dieser Zeit bin ich
sowie meine russ. Arbeitskameradin Natalia Nogeda aus Kiew
Ukreine sehr gut behandelt worden.Schläge gab es nie,das Essen
war sehr gut und konnte sich jederzeit sattessen. Wurde trotz
verbot am Tisch der Familie eingenommen. Gab es was Extras
bekamen wir auch davon. Schlafgelegenheit in guten Federbetten
Für Kleidung sorgte er ebenfalls neue markenfrei Sachen. Kurz in jeder Hinsicht
kann ich nur gutes sagen.Ich bitte die Familie jetzt auch
dementsprechent zu behandeln.

Note from Bella to Scheibes describing her
false identity during the war. No date. In German.

Made in the USA
Columbia, SC
12 June 2018